Ethical Decisions for Social Work Practice

Ralph Dolgoff

University of Maryland, Baltimore

Donna Harrington

University of Maryland, Baltimore

Frank M. Loewenberg

Emeritus, Bar-Ilan University

Prepared by

Peggy Proudfoot-McGuire

Salisbury University

✷ Cengage

Australia • Brazil • Canada • Mexico • Singapore • United Kingdom • United States

For product information and technology assistance, contact us at **Cengage Customer & Sales Support, 1-800-354-9706 or support.cengage.com.**

For permission to use material from this text or product, submit all requests online at **www.copyright.com**.

ISBN-13: 978-1-111-77193-5
ISBN-10: 1-111-77193-6

Cengage
200 Pier 4 Boulevard
Boston, MA 02210
USA

Cengage is a leading provider of customized learning solutions with employees residing in nearly 40 different countries and sales in more than 125 countries around the world. Find your local representative at: **www.cengage.com.**

To learn more about Cengage platforms and services, register or access your online learning solution, or purchase materials for your course, visit **www.cengage.com.**

Printed in the United States of America
Print Number: 06   Print Year: 2022

Contents

Empowerment Series

Dear Social Work Student,

Welcome to *Competencies/Practice Behaviors Workbook* for Dolgoff's *Ethical Decisions for Social Work Practice*, 9e. Throughout your course you will acquire a great deal of new knowledge, including an introduction to new theories, informative research, and practical skills like critical thinking skills and frameworks for appreciating and overcoming challenges. All of the knowledge you gain will offer you a deeper, richer understanding of social work. Used in conjunction with your text and other resources, the *Competencies/Practice Behaviors Workbook* presents you with Practice Exercises that will teach you how to transform your new knowledge into social work Practice Behaviors.

About Competence and Practice Behaviors

In social work, the words Competence and Practice Behavior have a unique meaning beyond the typical dictionary definitions. "Competence" in the usual sense means that a person possesses suitable skills and abilities to do a specific task. A competent baseball player must move quickly, catch, throw, and play as part of a team. They also have to think quickly, understand the rules of the game, and be knowledgeable of their environment. In the same way, a competent social worker should be able to do a number of job-related duties, think critically, and understand the context of their work. The Council on Social Work Education (CSWE) has defined specific Core Competency areas for all social work students, and their corresponding Practice Behaviors as follows:

Competencies and Practice Behaviors
2.1.1 Identify as a Professional Social Worker and Conduct Oneself Accordingly
a. Advocate for client access to the services of social work
b. Practice personal reflection and self-correction to assure continual professional development
c. Attend to professional roles and boundaries
d. Demonstrate professional demeanor in behavior, appearance, and communication
e. Engage in career-long learning
f. Use supervision and consultation
2.1.2 Apply Social Work Ethical Principles to Guide Professional Practice
a. Recognize and manage personal values in a way that allows professional values to guide practice
b. Make ethical decisions by applying standards of the National Association of Social Workers Code of Ethics and, as applicable, of the International Federation of Social Workers/ International Association of Schools of Social Work Ethics in Social Work, Statement of Principles

c.	Tolerate ambiguity in resolving ethical conflicts
d.	Apply strategies of ethical reasoning to arrive at principled decisions

2.1.3	**Apply Critical Thinking to Inform and Communicate Professional Judgments**
a.	Distinguish, appraise, and integrate multiple sources of knowledge, including research-based knowledge and practice wisdom
b.	Analyze models of assessment, prevention, intervention, and evaluation
c.	Demonstrate effective oral and written communication in working with individuals, families, groups, organizations, communities, and colleagues

2.1.4	**Engage Diversity and Difference in Practice**
a.	Recognize the extent to which a culture's structures and values may oppress, marginalize, alienate, or create or enhance privilege and power
b.	Gain sufficient self-awareness to eliminate the influence of personal biases and values in working with diverse groups
c.	Recognize and communicate their understanding of the importance of difference in shaping life experiences
d.	View themselves as learners and engage those with whom they work as informants

2.1.5	**Advance Human Rights and Social and Economic Justice**
a.	Understand the forms and mechanisms of oppression and discrimination
b.	Advocate for human rights and social and economic justice
c.	Engage in practices that advance social and economic justice

2.1.6	**Engage in Research-Informed Practice and Practice-Informed Research**
a.	Use practice experience to inform scientific inquiry
b.	Use research evidence to inform practice

2.1.7	**Apply Knowledge of Human Behavior and the Social Environment**
a.	Utilize conceptual frameworks to guide the processes of assessment, intervention, and evaluation
b.	Critique and apply knowledge to understand person and environment

2.1.8 to	**Engage in Policy Practice to Advance Social and Economic Well-Being and to Deliver Effective Social Work Services**
a.	Analyze, formulate, and advocate for policies that advance social well-being
b.	Collaborate with colleagues and clients for effective policy action

2.1.9	**Respond to Contexts that Shape Practice**
a.	Continuously discover, appraise, and attend to changing locales, populations, scientific and technological developments, and emerging societal trends to provide relevant services
b.	Provide leadership in promoting sustainable changes in service delivery and practice to improve the quality of social services

2.1.10	**Engage, Assess, Intervene, and Evaluate with Individuals, Families, Groups, Organizations and Communities**
a.	Substantively and affectively prepare for action with individuals, families, groups, organizations, and communities
b.	Use empathy and other interpersonal skills
c.	Develop a mutually agreed-on focus of work and desired outcomes
d.	Collect, organize, and interpret client data
e.	Assess client strengths and limitations

f.	Develop mutually agreed-on intervention goals and objectives
g.	Select appropriate intervention strategies
h.	Initiate actions to achieve organizational goals
i.	Implement prevention interventions that enhance client capacities
j.	Help clients resolve problems
k.	Negotiate, mediate, and advocate for clients
l.	Facilitate transitions and endings
m.	Critically analyze, monitor, and evaluate interventions

Each of the Exercises in the *Competencies/Practice Behaviors Workbook* will focus on learning and applying social work Practice Behaviors. While every Exercise will not ask you to apply Competencies or Practice Behaviors from every Core Competency area, by the time you finish your course you will have practiced many and gained a better working knowledge of how social work is done. The goal, shared by your professors, your program, the authors of this text, and by Brooks/Cole, Cengage Learning Social Work team, is that by the end of your curriculum you will have honed your Practice Behaviors in all of the Core Competency areas into a skill set that empowers you to work effectively as a professional social worker.

Assessing Competence: Partnering with Your Instructor and Peer Evaluator
As described above, the Council on Social Work Education clearly defines the Competencies and Practice Behaviors that a social work student should be trained to employ. Therefore, the grading rubric that comes at the end of every chapter of the *Competencies/Practice Behaviors Workbook* is adapted from Competencies and Practice Behaviors defined by CSWE (see the table above). To assess your competence during your course, we recommend you partner with a peer(s) who can act as your course "evaluator(s)" to genuinely assess both your written assignments and your role-plays; be sure to ask your professor to comment on and approve the assessments once they are completed by you and your Evaluator. It is our hope that partnering with your classmates in this way will familiarize you with the unique learning opportunity you will have in your Field Experience – the signature pedagogy of social work education. There you will apply all of your knowledge and skills under the supervision of your Field Instructor and Field Liaison before completing your required curriculum.

As always, we thank you for your commitment to education and to the profession. Enjoy your course, and *feel empowered to help others*!

Dolgoff's *Ethical Decisions for Social Work Practice, 9e* and *Competencies/Practice Behaviors Workbook* Aligned to EPAS 2008 Competencies and Practice Behaviors

Competencies and Practice Behaviors	Understanding Generalist Practice, 6e Chapters:	Practice Behaviors Workbook Practice Exercises:
2.1.1 Identify as a Professional Social Worker and Conduct Oneself Accordingly	1, 2, 3, 5, 6, 7, 8, 9, 10, 11, 12, 13	
a. Advocate for client access to the services of social work	5, 9, 12	1.1, 5.3, 11.1, 13.2
b. Practice personal reflection and self-correction to assure continual professional development	2, 5, 13	2.2, 13.2
c. Attend to professional roles and boundaries	7, 12	1.1, 2.5, 3.3, 5.3, 11.1, 13.2
d. Demonstrate professional demeanor in behavior, appearance, and communication		1.1, 2.2, 5.3, 11.1, 13.2
e. Engage in career-long learning		13.2
f. Use supervision and consultation		13.2
2.1.2 Apply Social Work Ethical Principles to Guide Professional Practice	1, 2, 3, 4, 5, 6, 7, 8, 9, 10, 11, 12, 13	
a. Recognize and manage personal values in a way that allows professional values to guide practice	2, 3, 4, 5, 6	12.5

b. Make ethical decisions by applying standards of the National Association of Social Workers Code of Ethics and, as applicable, of the International Federation of Social Workers/International Association of Schools of Social Work, Statement of Principles	1, 2, 3, 4, 5, 6, 7, 8, 9, 10, 11, 12, 13	1.5, 3.5, 11.5, 12.5
c. Tolerate ambiguity in resolving ethical conflicts	1, 2, 3, 4, 5, 6, 7, 8, 9, 10, 11, 12, 13	1.2, 2.1, 2.4, 12.5
d. Apply strategies of ethical reasoning to arrive at principled decisions	1, 2, 3, 4, 5, 6, 7, 8, 9, 10, 11, 12, 13	2.1, 2.3, 2.4, 3.2, 4.2, 4.3, 5.1, 5.2, 5.5, 6.1, 6.2, 6.3, 7.1, 7.2, 7.3, 7.4, 7.5, 8.2, 8.3, 8.4, 8.5, 9.1, 9.2, 9.4, 9.5, 10.2, 10.3, 10.4, 10.5, 11.2, 12.1, 12.3, 12.4, 12.5, 13.1, 13.3, 13.4
2.1.3 Apply Critical Thinking to Inform and Communicate Professional Judgments	1, 2, 3, 4, 5, 6, 7, 8, 9, 10, 11, 12, 13	
a. Distinguish, appraise, and integrate multiple sources of knowledge, including research-based knowledge and practice wisdom	1, 2, 3, 4, 5, 6, 7, 8, 9, 10, 11, 12, 13	1.3, 4.1, 4.4, 4.5, 5.4, 6.4, 6.5, 8.1, 10.1, 11.3, 13.5
b. Analyze models of assessment, prevention, intervention, and evaluation	12	1.3, 4.1, 4.4, 4.5, 5.4, 6.4, 6.5, 8.1, 10.1, 11.3, 13.5
c. Demonstrate effective oral and written communication in working with individuals, families, groups, organizations, communities, and colleagues	1, 2, 3, 4, 5, 6, 7, 8, 9, 10, 11, 12, 13	13.5
2.1.4 Engage Diversity and Difference in Practice	1, 2,3, 9, 11, 12	
a. Recognize the extent to which a culture's structures and values may oppress, marginalize, alienate, or create or enhance privilege and power	3, 6	

b.	Gain sufficient self-awareness to eliminate the influence of personal biases and values in working with diverse groups	2, 3, 6	1.4, 3.1, 3.4, 9.3, 11.4
c.	Recognize and communicate their understanding of the importance of difference in shaping life experiences	6	3.1
d.	View themselves as learners and engage those with whom they work as informants;		3.1
2.1.5	**Advance Human Rights and Social and Economic Justice**	9, 12	
a.	Understand forms and mechanisms of oppression and discrimination		12.2
b.	Advocate for human rights and social and economic justice	9, 12	12.2
c.	Engage in practices that advance social and economic justice	9, 12	12.2
2.1.6	**Engage in Research-Informed Practice and Practice-Informed Research**	12	
a.	Use practice experience to inform scientific inquiry	12	
b.	Use research evidence to inform practice	12	
2.1.7	**Apply Knowledge of Human Behavior and the Social Environment**		
a.	Utilize conceptual frameworks to guide the process of assessment, intervention, and evaluation		
b.	Critique and apply knowledge to understand person and environment		

2.1.8	**Engage in Policy Practice to Advance Social and Economic Well-Being and to Deliver Effective Social Work Services**			
a.	Analyze, formulate, and advocate for policies that advance social well-being			
b.	Collaborate with colleagues and clients for effective policy action			
2.1.9	**Respond to Contexts that Shape Practice**			
a.	Continuously discover, appraise, and attend to changing locales, populations, scientific and technological developments, and emerging societal trends to provide relevant services			
b.	Provide leadership in promoting sustainable changes in service delivery and practice to improve the quality of social services			
2.1.10	**Engage, Assess, Intervene, and Evaluate with Individuals, Families, Groups, Organizations and Communities**			
a.	Substantively and affectively prepare for action with individuals, families, groups, organizations, and communities			
b.	Use empathy and other interpersonal skills	1		
c.	Develop a mutually agreed-on focus of work and desired outcomes.			
d.	Collect, organize, and interpret client data			

X

e.	Assess client strengths and limitations							
f.	Develop mutually agreed-on intervention goals and objectives							
g.	Select appropriate intervention strategies							
h.	Initiate actions to achieve organizational goals							
i.	Implement prevention interventions that enhance client capacities							
j.	Help clients resolve problems							
k.	Negotiate, mediate, and advocate for clients							
l.	Facilitate transitions and endings							
m.	Critically analyze, monitor, and evaluate interventions							

Chapter 1

Ethical Choices in Helping Professions

Exercise 1: Practice in an Enmeshed Community

Focus Competencies/Practice Behaviors:

EP 2.1.1 Identify as a Professional Social Worker and Conduct Oneself Accordingly
a. Advocate for client access to the services of social work
c. Attend to professional roles and boundaries
d. Demonstrate professional demeanor in behavior, appearance, and communication

GOAL: *This exercise is designed to assist you in understanding how the social worker's value system, the value system of the employing agency and community affect the decision making process.*

> You have recently accepted a job in a state in which you are unfamiliar. You are a single parent with two school aged children and have finally found a nice tightly knit community in which you can afford to raise your children. The agency that has hired you is a Community Action Organization (CAO) containing many different components such as services for the homeless. You have been employed as a therapist for the mental health component and received a call from a local pediatrician referring two children ages 3 and 5. The pediatrician indicates that the children have been sexually abused, but Child Protective Services (CPS) in your community has not substantiated the case. Sexual abuse has been highly indicated by a medical expert at Children's Hospital and the pediatrician is seeking therapy for the children. You agree to take the case. As you are working with the children, you suspect that the abuse is continuing. The community is small and enmeshed and you find out that the administrator at CPS is related to the suspected perpetrator. The suspected perpetrator's family is very prominent in the community. You discuss the case with your supervisor and are immediately ordered to cease services because the CAO administrator is best friends with the suspected perpetrator's father. You are also given specific instructions by your supervisor not to report your suspicions to CPS. If you report to CPS your job is in jeopardy and there will probably not be an investigation anyway. Using Figure 1.1 from your text, begin the decision making process by outlining: The alternative decision making options from the scenario; who the participants are; and your assumptions about human nature, values etc. Think critically about each step in the process.

Exercise 2: Conflicting Values

Focus Competencies/Practice Behaviors:

EP 2.1.2 Apply Social Work Ethical Principles to Guide Professional Practice
c. Tolerate ambiguity in resolving ethical conflicts

1

GOAL: *This exercise is designed to assist you in understanding the types of dilemmas that arise in social work practice and several possible processes that you might employ to solve them. It is also designed to provide an example of tolerating ambiguity in resolving ethical conflicts.*

Imagine that you are a social worker at a community substance abuse center. A young woman who is an employee at the center has referred her fiancé' for services and he has been assigned to your case load. She asks you if he is HIV positive, but he has asked that the information remain confidential.

Step 1: Ask the students to read the chapter in the NASW Code of Ethics that discusses issues of confidentiality.

Step 2: Ask the students to read the guidelines involving "Duty to Warn."

Step 3: Divide students into two groups, one considering the scenario strictly by the NASW confidentiality standards and one considering the scenario strictly by the "Duty to Warn" standards. Stage a debate between the two sides utilizing the two opposing values.

Step 4: After the debate, discuss how the conflict can be resolved utilizing both standards and highlight that each case is unique and requires strategies of ethical reasoning to arrive at principled decisions.

Exercise 3: Critical Thinking

Focus Competencies/Practice Behaviors:

EP 2.1.3 Apply Critical Thinking to Inform and Communicate Professional Judgments
a. Distinguish, appraise, and integrate multiple sources of knowledge, including research based knowledge, and practice wisdom
b. Analyze models of assessment, prevention, intervention, and evaluations

GOAL: *This exercise highlights ethical dilemmas that can arise when conflicting groups assert privileges over the social worker's allegiance.*

> Imagine that you are a new social worker at a community mental health center that prescribes a Gestalt treatment modality in which you have been extensively trained. You have a client who has been diagnosed with Borderline Personality Disorder. Evidence indicates that Gestalt Therapy is not appropriate for clients with this issue, but your supervisor insists that you utilize the modality anyway because of the agency's reputation.

Step 1: Ask the students to discuss if the client or the agency should receive priority in their decision making process and discuss their reasons why.

Step 2: Students will individually outline the process which they will utilize in making their case for prioritizing the needs of the client or agency (approximately 10 minutes).

2

For example: Step 1 – gather evidence about the effects of Gestalt Therapy with Borderline Personality Disorder. Step 2 – analyze the evidence and communicate it effectively with supervisor, etc.

Step 3: Students will discuss their processes and the possible outcomes both for the person or agency as well as for themselves professionally.

Exercise 4: Diversity and Difference in Social Work Practice

Focus Competencies/Practice Behaviors:

EP 2.1.4 Engage diversity and difference in practice
b. Gain sufficient self-awareness to eliminate the influence of personal biases and values in working with diverse groups

GOAL: *This exercise is designed to help students gain sufficient awareness to eliminate the influence of personal biases and values when working with diverse clients.*

Imagine that you are a social worker working for a rural public health center. Although you are a professional, your salary is barely above the poverty guidelines. You have health insurance through the center, but the premiums and co-pays are very high. Recently you had to pay to have your three children immunized. You have recently been assigned to coordinate a health van which will provide health care services including immunizations to undocumented immigrants in the area. You believe that undocumented immigrants should be expelled from the United States or gain citizenship to stay in the country.

Step 1: Ask the students to discuss their feelings about providing services under the above circumstances.

Step 2: Explain to the students that tolerance needs to be observed during the discussion so that all opinions may be voiced. You will have diverse opinions during the discussion and should take into consideration all opinions EVEN IF they are not well thought out.

Step 3: After some discussion is generated ask the students to consider how they might feel being the clients who were brought to the United States by employers seeking cheap labor and now find themselves viewed as outcasts and unable to access even the most basic services such as health care.

Step 4: Students should research the guidelines for United States citizenship including the time frame. Ask students to write a one page paper describing what they might do under these circumstances. Returning to their country of origin is NOT AN OPTION.

Exercise 5: Varying Roles in Social Work Practice

Focus Competencies/Practice Behaviors:

EP 2.1.2 Apply social work ethical principles to guide professional practice
b. Make ethical decisions by applying standards of the National Association of Social Workers   Code of Ethics and, as applicable, of the International Federation of Social Workers/International Association of Schools of Social Work Ethics in Social Work, Statement of Principles.

GOAL: *This exercise is designed to help students begin to understand various ethical circumstances that might occur depending on the social work role.*

> Imagine that you are a social worker working for a federal public defender's office. Your title is "mitigation specialist" and you are required to work with clients who are being prosecuted for various offenses including murder. You are investigating a particular case and come into contact with a witness whom you believe might be perpetrating child abuse. You are a social worker and must follow the NASW Code of Ethics as a mandated reporter. However, your JOB specifies that you are an extension of the public defender and must adhere to attorney-client privilege which is equivalent to social worker – client confidentiality standards.

Step 1: Ask the students to consider to whom they owe their loyalties.

Step 2: Students should research the National Association of Forensic Social Workers guidelines as well as the NASW Code of Ethics.

Step 3: Ask students to discuss their opinions about the possibility of incongruities between the roles of social worker and the title of mitigation specialist with regard to tasks and functions.

4

Role-Play

Exercise A: Ethical and Professional Conduct in Court Situations

Focus Competencies/Practice Behaviors:

EP 2.1.2 Apply social work ethical principles to guide professional practice
a. Recognize and manage personal values in a way that allows professional values to guide   practice
d. Apply strategies of ethical reasoning to arrive at principled decisions

GOAL: *To demonstrate the application of social work ethical principles that guide professional practice.*

Step 1: The students assume that they are social workers for Child Protection Services. They have been working on a child sexual abuse case and have been called to testify at the court hearing on custody. Sexual abuse has been substantiated and the social worker is now being questioned by the alleged perpetrator's attorney. During questioning the attorney insinuates that the social worker has behaved unprofessionally with regard to boundary violations citing the opinion of a local mental health social worker. How should the social worker respond?
Step 2: Ask Students to review their State Social Work Code of Ethics and the NASW Code of Ethics regarding boundary issues with clients and professional conduct toward colleagues.
Step 3: Ask for volunteers to discuss boundary violations and professional conduct toward fellow social workers. Expand on this theme with several "what if" scenarios such as if the defense attorney states "your superior has accused you of behaving unprofessionally and violating professional boundaries with my client. What do you think about that?"
Step 4: Discuss possible alternatives such as the social worker stating "if she feels that way then she should file a complaint with our State Social Work Board."
Step 5: Have the students role play various scenarios.

5

Name: _____   **Date:** _____
Supervisor's Name: _____

Focus Competencies/Practice Behaviors:

EP 2.1.1 Identify as a Professional Social Worker and Conduct Oneself Accordingly
a. Advocate for client access to the services of social work
c. Attend to professional roles and boundaries
d. Demonstrate professional demeanor in behavior, appearance, and communication

EP 2.1.2 Apply Social Work Ethical Principles to Guide Professional Practice
b. Make ethical decisions by applying standards of the National Association of Social Workers
Code of Ethics and, as applicable, of the International Federation of Social Workers/International
Association of Schools of Social Work Ethics in Social Work, Statement of Principles.
c. Tolerate ambiguity in resolving ethical conflicts

EP 2.1.3 Apply Critical Thinking to Inform and Communicate Professional Judgments
a. Distinguish, appraise, and integrate multiple sources of knowledge, including   research based
knowledge, and practice wisdom
b. Analyze models of assessment, prevention, intervention, and evaluations

EP 2.1.4 Engage Diversity and Difference in Practice
a. Gain sufficient self-awareness to eliminate the influence of personal biases and values in
working with diverse groups

Instructions:

A.   Evaluate your work or your partner's work in the Focus Competencies/Practice
      Behaviors by completing the Competencies/Practice Behaviors Assessment form below
B.   What other Competencies/Practice Behaviors did you use to complete these Exercises?
      Be sure to record them in your assessments

1.	I have attained this competency/practice behavior (in the range of 81 to 100%)
2.	I have largely attained this competency/practice behavior (in the range of 61 to 80%)
3.	I have partially attained this competency/practice behavior (in the range of 41 to 60%)
4.	I have made a little progress in attaining this competency/practice behavior (in the range of 21 to 40%)
5.	I have made almost no progress in attaining this competency/practice behavior (in the range of 0 to 20%)

Student and Evaluator Assessment Scale and Comments	0	1	2	3	4	5	Agree/Disagree/Comments
EP 2.1.1 Identify as a Professional Social Worker and Conduct Oneself Accordingly							
a. Advocate for client access to the services of social work							
b. Practice personal reflection and self-correction to assure continual professional development							
c. Attend to professional roles and boundaries							
d. Demonstrate professional demeanor in behavior, appearance, and communication							
e. Engage in career-long learning							
f. Use supervision and consultation							
EP 2.1.2 Apply Social Work Ethical Principles to Guide Professional Practice							
a. Recognize and manage personal values in a way that allows professional values to guide practice							
b. Make ethical decisions by applying NASW Code of Ethics and, as applicable, of the IFSW/IASSW Ethics in Social Work, Statement of Principles							
c. Tolerate ambiguity in resolving ethical conflicts							
d. Apply strategies of ethical reasoning to arrive at principled decisions							

Student and Evaluator Assessment Scale and Comments	0	1	2	3	4	5	Agree/Disagree/Comments
EP 2.1.3 Apply Critical Thinking to Inform and Communicate Professional Judgments							
a. Distinguish, appraise, and integrate multiple sources of knowledge, including research-based knowledge and practice wisdom							
b. Analyze models of assessment, prevention, intervention, and evaluation							
c. Demonstrate effective oral and written communication in working with individuals, families, groups, organizations, communities, and colleagues							
EP 2.1.4 Engage Diversity and Difference in Practice							
a. Recognize the extent to which a culture's structures and values may oppress, marginalize, alienate, or create or enhance privilege and power							
b. Gain sufficient self-awareness to eliminate the influence of personal biases and values in working with diverse groups							
c. Recognize and communicate their understanding of the importance of difference in shaping life experiences							
d. View themselves as learners and engage those with whom they work as informants							

EP 2.1.5 Advance Human Rights and Social and Economic Justice							
a. Understand forms and mechanisms of oppression and discrimination							
b. Advocate for human rights and social and economic justice							
c. Engage in practices that advance social and economic justice							
EP 2.1.6 Engage in Research-Informed Practice and Practice-Informed Research							
a. Use practice experience to inform scientific inquiry							
b. Use research evidence to inform practice							
EP 2.1.7 Apply Knowledge of Human Behavior and the Social Environment							
a. Utilize conceptual frameworks to guide the processes of assessment, intervention, and evaluation							
b. Critique and apply knowledge to understand person and environment							
EP 2.1.8 Engage in Policy Practice to Advance Social and Economic Well-Being and to Deliver Effective Social Work Services							
a. Analyze, formulate, and advocate for policies that advance social well-being							
b. Collaborate with colleagues and clients for effective policy action							
EP 2.1.9 Respond to Contexts that Shape Practice							
a. Continuously discover, appraise, and attend to changing locales, populations, scientific and technological developments, and emerging societal trends to provide relevant services							
b. Provide leadership in promoting sustainable changes in service delivery and practice to improve the quality of social services							
EP 2.1.10 Engage, Assess, Intervene, and Evaluate with Individuals, Families, Groups, Organizations and Communities							
a. Substantively and affectively prepare for action with individuals, families, groups, organizations, and communities							
b. Use empathy and other interpersonal skills							
c. Develop a mutually agreed-on focus of work and desired outcomes							
d. Collect, organize, and interpret client data							
e. Assess client strengths and limitations							
f. Develop mutually agreed-on intervention goals and objectives							
g. Select appropriate intervention strategies							
h. Initiate actions to achieve organizational goals							
i. Implement prevention interventions that enhance client capacities							
j. Help clients resolve problems							
k. Negotiate, mediate, and advocate for clients							
l. Facilitate transitions and endings							
m. Critically analyze, monitor, and evaluate interventions							

8

Chapter 2

Values and Professional Ethics

Exercise 1: Complicated Decision Making

Focus Competencies/Practice Behaviors:

EP 2.1.2 Apply social work ethical principles to guide professional practice
c. Tolerate ambiguity in resolving ethical conflicts
d. Apply strategies of ethical reasoning to arrive at principled decisions

GOAL: *Codes of ethics generally provide guidance only for good/bad decisions. While common sense and sound ethical judgments are usually sufficient to guide social worker's choices, there are situations where good/good choices will always yield good results and bad/bad decisions will always yield unintended negative results. The following exercise is designed to provide an example of an ethical dilemma that is not oriented toward good/bad decision making.*

> John Miller is seriously mentally ill and has been so diagnosed by several psychiatrists. For the past three years, this 21-year-old adult has been living at home with his elderly parents. He can take care of his own minimal needs, but he has no interest whatsoever in any personal contact. He spends most of the day sitting in the living room, staring either into empty space or at the TV. His parents dare not leave him home alone. They have approached you, John's social worker, requesting that you make arrangements to have him returned to the state hospital because they feel they can no longer give him the care he needs. You appreciate their situation, but you also know that returning John to a state hospital may harm him.

Step 1: Write down specific circumstances that warrant hospitalization. For example: Does John's behavior indicate that he is a danger to himself or others?

Step 2: What resources are available in the area to assist John and his parents other than institutionalization?

Step 3: What ethical considerations are involved for John? What ethical considerations are involved from his parent's point of view?

Step 4: Does John's diagnosis warrant concern that he will possibly become dangerous in the future?

Step 5: Review the NASW Code of Ethics and find information that will help guide your ultimate decision.

Step 6: Share your findings with the class.

Exercise 2: Conflicting Values

Focus Competencies/Practice Behaviors:

EP 2.1.1 Identify as a professional social worker and conduct oneself accordingly
b. Practice personal reflection and self-correction to assure continual professional development
EP 2.1.2 Apply social work ethical principles to guide professional practice
d. Apply strategies of ethical reasoning to arrive at principled decisions

GOAL: *This exercise is designed to assist you in considering how your personal values affect the quality of your decision making and ultimately the services you provide as a social worker.*

> Imagine that you are a social worker working as a mitigation specialist for a public defender. You generally work on cases where the penalties for conviction range from probation to life sentences. However, you have been assigned to the Capital Habeas Unit to work on a post conviction case where the defendant has been sentenced to death. The circumstances of the crime are heinous, involving the murder of a two year old child. Even though you have been trained in social work to understand the consequences of the environment on human behavior, your religious background has influenced you to believe in good and evil. Personally, you see the client's acts as those involving evil and believe he should received the death penalty. You MUST take the case and need the job. How will you provide ethical services to this client?

Step 1: Write down what YOU BELIEVE the majority of society would consider to be the proper moral stance in this situation.

Step 2: Write down what you believe to be the proper moral stance.

Step 3: Write down a synopsis of possible mitigating circumstance that could have influenced the client to commit the heinous murder.

Step 4: Write down how you will use your knowledge of human development, theories of human behavior to include person in environment to help broaden your scope of cause and effect.

Step 5: Write down how you will balance your religious and social work values to proceed effectively with the investigation.

Exercise 3: Critical Thinking

Focus Competencies/Practice Behaviors:

E.P. 2.1.2 Apply social work ethical principles to guide professional practice
d. Apply strategies of ethical reasoning to arrive at principled decisions

GOAL: *This exercise highlights ethical dilemmas that can arise when you are practicing in a capacity that has a dual role of protective authority and family centered services such as in a child protective services agency.*

> Imagine that you are a new social worker at a child welfare agency. You have observed one of your colleagues who is a child sexual abuse investigator spend a great deal of time looking at material on the internet that is sexually provocative. He maintains that he is looking at the material in order to help him understand the nature of child sexual perpetrators. The child services agency is located in a small community and the investigator is highly regarded in the community and also practices as a minister of a local church. You are concerned about his behavior, but are also concerned about your own position, believing that you are in danger of losing your job if you report your concerns.

Step 1: Divide into two groups.

Step 2: Students will individually outline the process which they will utilize in defining their suspicions about their colleague (approximately 10 minutes). For example: What other evidence suggest that your colleague might be acting inappropriately?

Step 3: Define the alternatives with regard to reporting your suspicions. For example: Will you discuss your suspicions with a colleague prior to talking with your supervisor?

Step 4: Go to the NASW Code of Ethics and find the areas that speak to this dilemma

Step 5: As a group, decide on a course of action, come back together as a class and discuss your group's process and final decision(s).

Exercise 4: Diversity and Difference in Social Work Practice

Focus Competencies/Practice Behaviors:

EP 2.1.2 Apply social work ethical principles to guide professional practice
c. Tolerate ambiguity in resolving ethical conflicts
d. Apply strategies of ethical reasoning to arrive at principled decisions

GOAL: *This exercise is designed to help students gain sufficient awareness to eliminate the influence of personal biases and values when working with diverse clients.*

11

You work for an inner city mental health agency in a small Arizona town. Maria Chavez has been referred to your agency after being reported to child welfare for possible neglect of her four year old daughter. She works long hours as a maid and was reported as leaving her daughter alone during the day. She has been referred to you and is required to see you for counseling and for parent education as part of the plan to keep her child from going to a foster home. She tells you that the child welfare agency is requiring her to take her child to a day care, but that her husband who is an illegal alien and her daughter's father has actually been watching her during the day. She could not tell the child welfare worker about her husband for fear that he would be deported. You feel strongly that immigrants should be documented and are also concerned about repercussions from the state of Arizona if you do not report the situation. You are also concerned about your client's welfare and want her to maintain her daughter a home.

Step 1: Consult the NASW Code of Ethics and review the code(s) related to the situation. Consult the State and Federal laws related to the situation.

Step 2: Generate discussion among students about this situation and ask for opinions.

Step 3: During the last 15 minutes of class, ask students to develop a plan based on best practice.

Exercise 5: Varying Roles in Social Work Practice

Focus Competencies/Practice Behaviors:

EP 2.1.1 Identify as a professional social worker and conduct oneself accordingly
c. Attend to professional roles and boundaries

GOAL: *This exercise is designed to help students take into consideration situations which could be considered boundary violations.*

You are a social worker who is also a certified substance abuse counselor. One of your clients has asked that you allow him to put a roof on your house in exchange for services. His insurance has expired and he is not eligible for Medicaid. He is a licensed contractor and can pay with his roofing services.

Step 1: Consult the NASW Code of Ethics.

Step 2: Divide into two groups and discuss how the Code guides social workers in these situations.

Step 3: Think about alternatives that your client could consider for payment of services. Come back together to discuss your findings and what the best possible solutions might be.

Role-Play

Exercise A: Analysis of Personal Values and Understanding Laws Governing Client Requests

Focus Competencies/Practice Behaviors:

EP 2.1.1 Identify as a professional social worker and conduct oneself accordingly
a. Advocate for client access to the services of social work;
b. Practice personal reflection and self-correction to assure continual professional development

GOAL: *To demonstrate the application of social work ethical principles that guide professional practice.*

Step 1: You are a social worker at a mental health center. One of your teen aged clients has revealed to you that she is pregnant and plans on having an abortion. She is 14 years old and has asked you not to tell her parents. You do not believe in abortion and would prefer to guide your client to a center that advocates for having the child and an alternative such as adoption.

Step 2: Have students choose the role of the social worker and the client and role play this situation. Ask them to reverse roles. Have students write down their opinions of the role play and dismiss them to return to the role play during the next class.

Step 3: For homework, ask students to find their state's laws governing revealing information to parents of a minor. Also, ask them to find out the guidelines of agencies in the area governing confidentiality of information revealed by a minor.

Step 4: Additional homework: Ask students to write down their own values about abortion and how their values might influence their work with this client.

Step 5: Re-convene the class and with the new information ask them to repeat the role plays with other partners.

Step 6: Ask the class to discuss the role play before and after gaining understanding of the rules and their own values.

Name: _____ **Date:** _____

Supervisor's Name: _____

Focus Competencies/Practice Behaviors:

EP 2.1.1 Identify as a Professional Social Worker and Conduct Oneself Accordingly
b. Practice personal reflection and self-correction to assure continual professional development
c. Attend to professional roles and boundaries

EP 2.1.2 Apply Social Work Ethical Principles to Guide Professional Practice
a. Tolerate ambiguity in resolving ethical conflicts
b. Apply strategies of ethical reasoning to arrive at principled decisions
c. Tolerate ambiguity in resolving ethical conflicts
d. Apply strategies of ethical reasoning to arrive at principled decisions

Instructions:

A.   Evaluate your work or your partner's work in the Focus Competencies/Practice Behaviors by completing the Competencies/Practice Behaviors Assessment form below

B.   What other Competencies/Practice Behaviors did you use to complete these Exercises? Be sure to record them in your assessments

1.	I have attained this competency/practice behavior (in the range of 81 to 100%)
2.	I have largely attained this competency/practice behavior (in the range of 61 to 80%)
3.	I have partially attained this competency/practice behavior (in the range of 41 to 60%)
4.	I have made a little progress in attaining this competency/practice behavior (in the range of 21 to 40%)
5.	I have made almost no progress in attaining this competency/practice behavior (in the range of 0 to 20%)

Student and Evaluator Assessment Scale and Comments	0	1	2	3	4	5	Agree/Disagree/Comments
EP 2.1.1 Identify as a Professional Social Worker and Conduct Oneself Accordingly							
a. Advocate for client access to the services of social work							
b. Practice personal reflection and self-correction to assure continual professional development							
c. Attend to professional roles and boundaries							
d. Demonstrate professional demeanor in behavior, appearance, and communication							
e. Engage in career-long learning							
f. Use supervision and consultation							

EP 2.1.2 Apply Social Work Ethical Principles to Guide Professional Practice							
a.	Recognize and manage personal values in a way that allows professional values to guide practice						
b.	Make ethical decisions by applying NASW Code of Ethics and, as applicable, of the IFSW/IASSW Ethics in Social Work, Statement of Principles						
c.	Tolerate ambiguity in resolving ethical conflicts						
d.	Apply strategies of ethical reasoning to arrive at principled decisions						

EP 2.1.3 Apply Critical Thinking to Inform and Communicate Professional Judgments							
a.	Distinguish, appraise, and integrate multiple sources of knowledge, including research-based knowledge and practice wisdom						
b.	Analyze models of assessment, prevention, intervention, and evaluation						
c.	Demonstrate effective oral and written communication in working with individuals, families, groups, organizations, communities, and colleagues						
EP 2.1.4 Engage Diversity and Difference in Practice							
a.	Recognize the extent to which a culture's structures and values may oppress, marginalize, alienate, or create or enhance privilege and power						
b.	Gain sufficient self-awareness to eliminate the influence of personal biases and values in working with diverse groups						
c.	Recognize and communicate their understanding of the importance of difference in shaping life experiences						
d.	View themselves as learners and engage those with whom they work as informants						

EP 2.1.5 Advance Human Rights and Social and Economic Justice							
a.	Understand forms and mechanisms of oppression and discrimination						
b.	Advocate for human rights and social and economic justice						
c.	Engage in practices that advance social and economic justice						
EP 2.1.6 Engage in Research-Informed Practice and Practice-Informed Research							
a.	Use practice experience to inform scientific inquiry						
b.	Use research evidence to inform practice						

EP 2.1.7 Apply Knowledge of Human Behavior and the Social Environment							
a.	Utilize conceptual frameworks to guide the processes of assessment, intervention, and evaluation						
b.	Critique and apply knowledge to understand person and environment						
EP 2.1.8 Engage in Policy Practice to Advance Social and Economic Well-Being and to Deliver Effective Social Work Services							
a.	Analyze, formulate, and advocate for policies that advance social well-being						
b.	Collaborate with colleagues and clients for effective policy action						
EP 2.1.9 Respond to Contexts that Shape Practice							
a.	Continuously discover, appraise, and attend to changing locales, populations, scientific and technological developments, and emerging societal trends to provide relevant services						
b.	Provide leadership in promoting sustainable changes in service delivery and practice to improve the quality of social services						
EP 2.1.10 Engage, Assess, Intervene, and Evaluate with Individuals, Families, Groups, Organizations and Communities							
a.	Substantively and affectively prepare for action with individuals, families, groups, organizations, and communities						
b.	Use empathy and other interpersonal skills						
c.	Develop a mutually agreed-on focus of work and desired outcomes						
d.	Collect, organize, and interpret client data						
e.	Assess client strengths and limitations						
f.	Develop mutually agreed-on intervention goals and objectives						
g.	Select appropriate intervention strategies						
h.	Initiate actions to achieve organizational goals						
i.	Implement prevention interventions that enhance client capacities						
j.	Help clients resolve problems						
k.	Negotiate, mediate, and advocate for clients						
l.	Facilitate transitions and endings						
m.	Critically analyze, monitor, and evaluate interventions						

16

Chapter 3

Guidelines for Ethical Decision Making: Concepts, Approaches, and Values

Exercise 1: Agreement with Death

Focus Competencies/Practice Behaviors:

EP 2.1.4 Engage diversity and difference in practice
b. Gain sufficient self-awareness to eliminate the influence of personal biases and values in working with diverse groups
c. Recognize and communicate their understanding of the importance of difference in shaping life experiences
d. View themselves as learners and engage those with whom they work as informants

GOAL: *Social workers appreciate that, as a consequence of difference, a person's life experiences may include oppression, poverty, marginalization, and alienation as well as privilege, power, and acclaim. Social workers understand how diversity characterizes and shapes the human experience and is critical to the formation of identity. This exercise is designed to increase the social worker's self-awareness of values and personal biases In working with the terminally ill. It is also designed to help social workers recognize the importance of difference in shaping clients.*

Jake Overton is a 55 year old bi-racial gay male. He is a successful artist and is in the final phases of HIV/AIDS. He found out he was HIV positive 20 years ago and has valiantly engaged in every medical intervention available. He presently weights 90 lbs, has tuberculosis, and has a feeding tube and catheter. Although Jakes prognosis is not good, there is a slim possibility that he could rally or that a new drug could be developed which would prolong his life. You are a hospice social worker in Oregon where patients legally have the right to terminate their lives. This law violates your professional and personal values. Jake has asked that you as his social worker help him arrange suicide. He has conveyed to you his wishes and knows that you can begin advocating and arranging for his wishes to be carried out. You can ask that another social worker take the case, but you have developed a close relationship with Jake and he has specifically requested that you act on his behalf.

Step 1: Review Chapter 3 on ethical decision making and decide which ethical principal(s) you will base you decision on.

Step 2: Write down the ethical principal(s) that you have chosen and explain your choice(s).

Step 3: Ask each student to discuss his/her choice(s) and reasoning.

Step 4: Ask each student to discuss their decision to help or not help their client.

17

Step 5: If a student decides not to attend to the client's wishes, ask them to discuss how they will handle the situation.

Exercise 2: Theoretically Guided Decision Making

Focus Competencies/Practice Behaviors:

EP 2.1.2 Apply social work ethical principles to guide professional practice
d. Apply strategies of ethical reasoning to arrive at principled decisions

GOAL: *To understand how theoretical perspectives influence decision making.*

> As a social worker in a mental health center that contracts with the local children's services agency you have been assigned to a child protective services (CPS) case working with a family who has been identified as being high risk for neglect. You are working with a single mother and her three adolescent children. The mother works at a full time job and depends on the oldest child who is 12 to make sure that the younger children ages 9 and 7 are fed and taken care of after school until she returns home. The child protective services worker has a part-time job as a law enforcement officer in the area and had knowledge that the estranged husband and father of the family had an outstanding warrant for his arrest. This worker decided to go to your client's home during his role as a CPS worker to "check" on the family but primarily to see if the father was at the home. He found the oldest child caring for the youngest children and filed a report asserting neglect. He tells you that he is truly concerned about the children's wellbeing although he did not find any evidence of neglect. He also tells you that he substantiated the neglect charges in order to "keep an eye" out for the father who is in trouble with the law. The CPS worker is well known in the community and highly respected within the children's services agency and in the law enforcement community.

Step 1: Review the guidelines for acting as an ethical relativist.

Step 2: Review the guidelines for acting as an ethical absolutist.

Step 3: Write down your ideas of how you would handle this situation from each perspective.

Step 4: Divide into groups: One group representing the ethical relativist perspective and one group representing the ethical absolutist perspective. Decide how your group will handle the situation.

Step 5: After discussing your respective strategies, come back together as a group and discuss your findings.

18

Exercise 3: Boundary Issues

Focus Competencies/Practice Behaviors:

E.P. 2.1.1 Identify as a Professional Social Worker and Conduct Oneself Accordingly
c. Attend to professional roles and boundaries

GOAL: *As noted in your text every social worker needs tools of analysis that will permit a more systematic and rational consideration of the ethical aspects of social work intervention.*

A clinical social worker provided expert testimony in court in conjunction with a suit filed by parents of a child diagnosed with autism. The parents alleged negligence and incompetence in the earlier treatment of their child by another psychotherapist. Now the parents have requested that the social worker become the treating therapist for their child. The social worker acknowledges that he probably has more expertise in the field than anyone in the area. He is concerned that if he does not agree to treat the child, the child could possibly be denied of the best services available. However, he is aware that if he does agree to treat the child, his actions could be considered to be a conflict of interest because he profited from being the court-appointed assessor (NASW, 1998).

Step 1: Return to Chapter 3 in you text and review the ethical models for decision making. Recall that as social workers we emphasize rational, scientific, and systematic decision making models.

Step 2: Consider each model and decide on two models that you consider to have incorporated a rational, scientific, and systematic approach.

Step 3: Write a two page paper outlining your priorities in this case based on each model. You may prioritize based on the guidelines under the Critical Thinking Exercise at the end of Chapter 3.

Exercise 4: Influence of Personal Values

Focus Competencies/Practice Behaviors:

EP 2.1.4 Engage diversity and difference in practice
b. Gain sufficient self-awareness to eliminate the influence of personal biases and values in working with diverse groups

GOAL: *This exercise is designed to challenge students to identify personal bias in practice.*

As a social worker practicing in substance abuse, you encounter many different clients including transgendered clients. You have been assigned to counsel a transgendered client who is actively engaged in heroin addiction and is HIV positive. Your best friend recently died of complications associated with HIV. She unknowingly engaged in a relationship with an HIV positive partner who ultimately disserted her when he found out that she became HIV positive. In addition, you have an aversion to transgendered individuals, believing that their choices go against "God's will." The agency is small and there is no-one with your expertise to counsel this individual. Additionally, there are scant substance abuse resources in your area.

Step 1: Assuming the role of this social worker, define your values about this situation clearly.

Step 2: What do you believe should happen to someone who goes against "God's will?" Do you believe that this individual deserves help or possibly is being punished for being a "deviant"?

Step 3: How might your own experience with your friend's death influence your treatment of this client?

Step 4: Break up into dyads. With your personal values clearly outlined, discuss how you would handle this situation with a classmate. Come back together as a class and discuss this situation, your values (as the social worker in the situation) and how you would handle this issue.

Exercise 5: Influence of Group Values

Focus Competencies/Practice Behaviors:

EP 2.1.2 Apply social work ethical principles to guide professional practice
b. Make ethical decisions by applying standards of the National Association of Social Workers Code of Ethics and, as applicable, of the International Federation of Social Workers/International Association of Schools of Social Work Ethics in Social Work, Statement of Principles.

GOAL: *This exercise is designed to help students begin to understand various ethical circumstances, the outcomes of which will depend on the values of the social worker.*

As a hospice social worker who deals with death and dying you are knowledgeable about the process of grief associated with the death of a loved one. However, you are working with a client whose young husband died suddenly. You believe she is working through her grief and has displayed a great deal of strength in coping with settling her husband's affairs. During one of the last sessions with you she breaks down and tells you that she has decided to commit suicide because she cannot tolerate the pain of being without the love of her life. She has a solid plan, and has no symptoms of psychosis or disorientation. Her reasoning is that she cannot take the psychological pain anymore. She tells you that you cannot talk her out of this, and if you report her she will deny that she told you.

20

Step 1: Prepare to speak to your supervisor about the situation and answer the following questions on a notepad to bring to the meeting:

1. What are your obligations to this client?
2. What is the harm/benefit ratio to others involved with this client?
3. What is the harm/benefit ratio to you as the client's therapist?
4. What is the social worker's duty to protect? Whom should be protected?
5. Are their costs to the agency?
6. How does your own value system speak to this situation with regard to religion, politics, etc.

Role-Play

Exercise A: Ethical and Professional Conduct in Court Situations Focus Competencies or Practice Behaviors

Focus Competencies/Practice Behaviors:

EP 2.1.2 Apply social work ethical principles to guide professional practice
a. Recognize and manage personal values in a way that allows professional values to guide practice
d. Apply strategies of ethical reasoning to arrive at principled decisions

GOAL: *To demonstrate the application of social work ethical principles that guide professional practice.*

Step 1: Using the scenario from Exercise 5, divide up into dyads in class. One student should role play the social work supervisor and the other should play the social worker. Reverse roles.

Step 3: Discuss your interactions with the class.

Name: _____ **Date:** _____

Supervisor's Name: _____

Focus Competencies/Practice Behaviors:

E.P. 2.1.1 Identify as a Professional Social Worker and Conduct Oneself Accordingly
c. Attend to professional roles and boundaries

EP 2.1.2 Apply social work ethical principles to guide professional practice
a. Recognize and manage personal values in a way that allows professional values to guide practice
b. Make ethical decisions by applying standards of the National Association of Social Workers Code of Ethics and, as applicable, of the International Federation of Social Workers/International Association of Schools of Social Work Ethics in Social Work, Statement of Principles.
d. Apply strategies of ethical reasoning to arrive at principled decisions

EP 2.1.4 Engage diversity and difference in practice
b. Gain sufficient self-awareness to eliminate the influence of personal biases and values in working with diverse groups
c. Recognize and communicate their understanding of the importance of difference in shaping life experiences
d. View themselves as learners and engage those with whom they work as informants

Instructions:

A.   Evaluate your work or your partner's work in the Focus Competencies/Practice Behaviors by completing the Competencies/Practice Behaviors Assessment form below
B.   What other Competencies/Practice Behaviors did you use to complete these Exercises? Be sure to record them in your assessments

1.	I have attained this competency/practice behavior (in the range of 81 to 100%)
2.	I have largely attained this competency/practice behavior (in the range of 61 to 80%)
3.	I have partially attained this competency/practice behavior (in the range of 41 to 60%)
4.	I have made a little progress in attaining this competency/practice behavior (in the range of 21 to 40%)
5.	I have made almost no progress in attaining this competency/practice behavior (in the range of 0 to 20%)

Student and Evaluator Assessment Scale and Comments	0	1	2	3	4	5	Agree/Disagree/Comments
EP 2.1.1 Identify as a Professional Social Worker and Conduct Oneself Accordingly							
a. Advocate for client access to the services of social work							
b. Practice personal reflection and self-correction to assure continual professional development							
c. Attend to professional roles and boundaries							
d. Demonstrate professional demeanor in behavior, appearance, and communication							
e. Engage in career-long learning							
f. Use supervision and consultation							
EP 2.1.2 Apply Social Work Ethical Principles to Guide Professional Practice							
a. Recognize and manage personal values in a way that allows professional values to guide practice							
b. Make ethical decisions by applying NASW Code of Ethics and, as applicable, of the IFSW/IASSW Ethics in Social Work, Statement of Principles							
c. Tolerate ambiguity in resolving ethical conflicts							
d. Apply strategies of ethical reasoning to arrive at principled decisions							

Student and Evaluator Assessment Scale and Comments	0	1	2	3	4	5	Agree/Disagree/Comments
EP 2.1.3 Apply Critical Thinking to Inform and Communicate Professional Judgments							
a. Distinguish, appraise, and integrate multiple sources of knowledge, including research-based knowledge and practice wisdom							
b. Analyze models of assessment, prevention, intervention, and evaluation							
c. Demonstrate effective oral and written communication in working with individuals, families, groups, organizations, communities, and colleagues							
EP 2.1.4 Engage Diversity and Difference in Practice							
a. Recognize the extent to which a culture's structures and values may oppress, marginalize, alienate, or create or enhance privilege and power							
b. Gain sufficient self-awareness to eliminate the influence of personal biases and values in working with diverse groups							
c. Recognize and communicate their understanding of the importance of difference in shaping life experiences							
d. View themselves as learners and engage those with whom they work as informants							

EP 2.1.5 Advance Human Rights and Social and Economic Justice							
a. Understand forms and mechanisms of oppression and discrimination							
b. Advocate for human rights and social and economic justice							
c. Engage in practices that advance social and economic justice							
EP 2.1.6 Engage in Research-Informed Practice and Practice-Informed Research							
a. Use practice experience to inform scientific inquiry							
b. Use research evidence to inform practice							
EP 2.1.7 Apply Knowledge of Human Behavior and the Social Environment							
a. Utilize conceptual frameworks to guide the processes of assessment, intervention, and evaluation							
b. Critique and apply knowledge to understand person and environment							
EP 2.1.8 Engage in Policy Practice to Advance Social and Economic Well-Being and to Deliver Effective Social Work Services							
a. Analyze, formulate, and advocate for policies that advance social well-being							
b. Collaborate with colleagues and clients for effective policy action							
EP 2.1.9 Respond to Contexts that Shape Practice							
a. Continuously discover, appraise, and attend to changing locales, populations, scientific and technological developments, and emerging societal trends to provide relevant services							
b. Provide leadership in promoting sustainable changes in service delivery and practice to improve the quality of social services							
EP 2.1.10 Engage, Assess, Intervene, and Evaluate with Individuals, Families, Groups, Organizations and Communities							
a. Substantively and affectively prepare for action with individuals, families, groups, organizations, and communities							
b. Use empathy and other interpersonal skills							
c. Develop a mutually agreed-on focus of work and desired outcomes							
d. Collect, organize, and interpret client data							
e. Assess client strengths and limitations							
f. Develop mutually agreed-on intervention goals and objectives							
g. Select appropriate intervention strategies							
h. Initiate actions to achieve organizational goals							
i. Implement prevention interventions that enhance client capacities							
j. Help clients resolve problems							
k. Negotiate, mediate, and advocate for clients							
l. Facilitate transitions and endings							
m. Critically analyze, monitor, and evaluate interventions							

Chapter 4

Guidelines for Ethical Decision Making: Decision Making Process and Tools

Exercise 1: Complete Confidentiality: Is It Real?

Focus Competencies/Practice Behaviors:

EP 2.1.3 Apply Critical Thinking to Inform and Communicate Professional Judgments
a. Distinguish, appraise, and integrate multiple sources of knowledge, including research based knowledge, and practice wisdom
b. Analyze models of assessment, prevention, intervention, and evaluations

GOAL: *Changing definitions of rights are likely to create ethical problems for social workers. Consider the ethical problems faced by social workers when states pass legislation that negates contracts that they have made with their clients. The goal of this exercise is to use the Ethical Assessment Screen (figure 4.2) from your text to clarify and integrate information to help in the decision making process.*

At one time, the biological and adoptive parents of adoptees were assured that private information would remain confidential and would never be shared with the adoptee. Presently, the right of adopted persons to information about their biological parents is becoming recognized in more and more jurisdictions. At one time, the biological and adoptive parents were assured that such information would remain confidential and would never be shared with the adoptee. Since court decisions or legislative enactments in some states now guarantee the right of adopted persons to this information, social workers in these jurisdictions may have little choice but to reveal this information, even though they had earlier, in good faith, assured both the biological and adoptive parents that this information would remain confidential. Is it ethical for social workers in states that have not yet passed such legislation to continue to tell biological and adoptive parents that this information will always remain confidential?

Step 1: Review figure 4.2 (Ethical Assessment Screen) from your text.

Step 2: Use the EAS to process the situation.

Step 3: Share your assessment with your classmates.

Exercise 2: Role Conflict and Ethical Dilemmas

Focus Competencies/Practice Behaviors:

EP 2.1.2 Apply social work ethical principles to guide professional practice
d. Apply strategies of ethical reasoning to arrive at principled decisions

GOAL: *To understand the responsibilities of the social worker as an agent of social control versus an agent of caring.*

You are a social worker in a small community mental health center. Your role is to work with juveniles who have been adjudicated delinquent. You have been working with a young man who has not been attending school and who has been charged with assault. You have been working with his family who is receiving public assistance and find out that his father has been running an illegal gambling (bookie) business out of his house. The family always appears to have plenty of money, but constantly uses food stamps, medical card, etc. Your client is aware of this and thinks that it is funny and cannot understand why his "crimes" are being punished since no one prosecutes his father.

Step 1: Weigh your obligations to your client against your obligations to his family and to society.

Step 2: To which function should you give priority if you cannot pursue both at the same time?

Step 3: Does it matter whether the father's behavior harms his wife and children? Can his behavior be overlooked if his son is making progress toward attaining identified and constructive intervention goals?

Step 4: Divide into groups of three. Discuss this case, write down your answers and share with your classmates.

Exercise 3: Security or Protection

Focus Competencies/Practice Behaviors:

E.P. 2.1.2 Apply social work ethical principles to guide professional practice
d. Apply strategies of ethical reasoning to arrive at principled decisions

GOAL: *As noted in your text every social worker must use problem solving skills to balance issues regarding the best interest of the client.*

John Newton is a likable young man—22 years old, not steadily employed, but always willing to help. Even before Ray Dunkirk, the community worker, had arrived on the scene, John had organized a number of young adults into a club. This club was well known in the neighborhood for the many helpful services it provided. The community's elderly population was especially appreciative of the security services that the group gave them. Thefts and holdups of older people had ceased ever since this club began to operate in the community. However, Ray became aware that John had intimidated local store owners and obtained regular payoffs from them in return for promising them ''protection.''

Step 1: Divide into two groups. Use the Ethical Rules Screen (figure 4.3) from your text.

Step 2: Analyze the above scenario using the ERS.

Step 3: Both groups should discuss their findings with each other during class.

Exercise 4: Effectiveness vs. Efficiency

Focus Competencies/Practice Behaviors:

EP 2.1.3 Apply Critical Thinking to Inform and Communicate Professional Judgments
a. Distinguish, appraise, and integrate multiple sources of knowledge, including research based knowledge, and practice wisdom
b. Analyze models of assessment, prevention, intervention, and evaluations

GOAL: *This exercise is designed for social workers to consider least harm and quality of life in their decision making.*

Jimmy Prego is a passive, deeply disturbed early adolescent. He lives in a therapeutic home where he has sometimes had to be protected from other residents. Now he is ready to be moved to a less restrictive environment. A therapeutic foster home, something your supervisor originally suggested, seems like the optimum solution. You have contacted such a home and begun plans to move Jimmy in about two weeks. When you inform your supervisor that you have initiated the move and that everything is proceeding routinely, she tells you that space has become available in an even less restricted group home run by your agency and that it would be appropriate to move Jimmy to the group home instead of the therapeutic foster home. You tell your supervisor that you will check it out, but she seems a little uncomfortable. When you check out the group home, you discover that the residents are older, bigger, and more aggressive than Jimmy. You inform your supervisor that this group home is definitely not appropriate for a boy like Jimmy, who already has had difficulties defending himself where he currently resides. At the same time, you become aware that the agency has placed pressure on all supervisors to boost the group home's census, an action related to agency financial situation. Jimmy's mother is unable to assist in making a decision about his placement because of her overwhelming personal and mental health problems. Jimmy's problems and his age make it unlikely that he is capable of making the decision. Mrs. Prego, his mother, insists that she trusts you and trusts that you will do what is best for Jimmy.

Step 1: Divide into groups of 2

Step 2: You have both ERS (figure 4.2) and EPS (figure 4.3) from your text to use to analyze this scenario.

Step 3: Remember that ERS should always be used first. However, ERS might not provide you with an exhaustive process and you may have to employ EPS.

Step 4: Write a paper about the process (es) you utilized with an explanation of why you chose the process (es).

27

Exercise 5: Withholding Medically Indicated Treatment from Disabled Infants with Life Threatening Conditions

Focus Competencies/Practice Behaviors:

EP 2.1.3 Apply Critical Thinking to Inform and Communicate Professional Judgments
a. Distinguish, appraise, and integrate multiple sources of knowledge, including research based knowledge, and practice wisdom
b. Analyze models of assessment, prevention, intervention, and evaluations

GOAL: *This exercise is designed to help students begin to understand dilemmas from a client and societal perspective, the outcomes of which will be based on the social worker's values and decision making process.*

> You are a social worker at a hospital Neonatal Intensive Care Unit. A young couple has just delivered a baby who is experiencing Down syndrome. The baby also has stomach issues which will require very risky and expensive surgery for which experts will have to be flown in. If the surgery is not done, the baby will die a slow and painful death. The couple's insurance will not pay for the surgery and the doctors indicate that the chances of the baby surviving the surgery are minimal. The parents do not want the baby to have the surgery. They are horrified at the prospect of having a child with developmental disabilities. As the social worker, what should you do?

Step 1: Use ERS (figure 4.2) and EPS (figure 4.3) from your text and begin to rank order the principles from the most important to the least important.

Step 2: Research any laws that pertain to a situation like this one.

Step 3: For a grade, write a paper outlining your process and the decisions you will make.

Role-Play

Exercise A: Ethical Conduct in a Tragic Situation

Focus Competencies/Practice Behaviors:

EP 2.1.2—Apply social work ethical principles to guide professional practice
a. Recognize and manage personal values in a way that allows professional values to guide practice
d. Apply strategies of ethical reasoning to arrive at principled decisions

GOAL: *To demonstrate the application of social work ethical principles that guide professional practice.*

Step 1: Using the scenario from Exercise 5, divide into groups of three. One student should role play the social worker and two students should role play the parents of the child.

Step 3: Discuss your interactions with the class.
.

Chapter 4

Competencies/Practice Behaviors Exercises Assessment:

Name: _____ **Date:** _____

Supervisor's Name: _____

Focus Competencies/Practice Behaviors:

EP 2.1.2 Apply Social Work Ethical Principles to Guide Professional Practice
a. Recognize and manage personal values in a way that allows professional values to guide practice
d. Apply strategies of ethical reasoning to arrive at principled decisions

EP 2.1.3 Apply Critical Thinking to Inform and Communicate Professional Judgments
a. Distinguish, appraise, and integrate multiple sources of knowledge, including research based knowledge, and practice wisdom
b. Analyze models of assessment, prevention, intervention, and evaluations

Instructions:

A.   Evaluate your work or your partner's work in the Focus Competencies/Practice Behaviors by completing the Competencies/Practice Behaviors Assessment form below
B.   What other Competencies/Practice Behaviors did you use to complete these Exercises? Be sure to record them in your assessments

1.	I have attained this competency/practice behavior (in the range of 81 to 100%)
2.	I have largely attained this competency/practice behavior (in the range of 61 to 80%)
3.	I have partially attained this competency/practice behavior (in the range of 41 to 60%)
4.	I have made a little progress in attaining this competency/practice behavior (in the range of 21 to 40%)
5.	I have made almost no progress in attaining this competency/practice behavior (in the range of 0 to 20%)

Student and Evaluator Assessment Scale and Comments	0	1	2	3	4	5	Agree/Disagree/Comments
EP 2.1.1 Identify as a Professional Social Worker and Conduct Oneself Accordingly							
a. Advocate for client access to the services of social work							
b. Practice personal reflection and self-correction to assure continual professional development							
c. Attend to professional roles and boundaries							
d. Demonstrate professional demeanor in behavior, appearance, and communication							
e. Engage in career-long learning							
f. Use supervision and consultation							

EP 2.1.2 Apply Social Work Ethical Principles to Guide Professional Practice							
a.	Recognize and manage personal values in a way that allows professional values to guide practice						
b.	Make ethical decisions by applying NASW Code of Ethics and, as applicable, of the IFSW/IASSW Ethics in Social Work, Statement of Principles						
c.	Tolerate ambiguity in resolving ethical conflicts						
d.	Apply strategies of ethical reasoning to arrive at principled decisions						

EP 2.1.3 Apply Critical Thinking to Inform and Communicate Professional Judgments							
a.	Distinguish, appraise, and integrate multiple sources of knowledge, including research-based knowledge and practice wisdom						
b.	Analyze models of assessment, prevention, intervention, and evaluation						
c.	Demonstrate effective oral and written communication in working with individuals, families, groups, organizations, communities, and colleagues						
EP 2.1.4 Engage Diversity and Difference in Practice							
a.	Recognize the extent to which a culture's structures and values may oppress, marginalize, alienate, or create or enhance privilege and power						
b.	Gain sufficient self-awareness to eliminate the influence of personal biases and values in working with diverse groups						
c.	Recognize and communicate their understanding of the importance of difference in shaping life experiences						
d.	View themselves as learners and engage those with whom they work as informants						
EP 2.1.5 Advance Human Rights and Social and Economic Justice							
a.	Understand forms and mechanisms of oppression and discrimination						
b.	Advocate for human rights and social and economic justice						
c.	Engage in practices that advance social and economic justice						
EP 2.1.6 Engage in Research-Informed Practice and Practice-Informed Research							
a.	Use practice experience to inform scientific inquiry						
b.	Use research evidence to inform practice						

31

EP 2.1.7 Apply Knowledge of Human Behavior and the Social Environment							
a. Utilize conceptual frameworks to guide the processes of assessment, intervention, and evaluation							
b. Critique and apply knowledge to understand person and environment							
EP 2.1.8 Engage in Policy Practice to Advance Social and Economic Well-Being and to Deliver Effective Social Work Services							
a. Analyze, formulate, and advocate for policies that advance social well-being							
b. Collaborate with colleagues and clients for effective policy action							
EP 2.1.9 Respond to Contexts that Shape Practice							
a. Continuously discover, appraise, and attend to changing locales, populations, scientific and technological developments, and emerging societal trends to provide relevant services							
b. Provide leadership in promoting sustainable changes in service delivery and practice to improve the quality of social services							
EP 2.1.10 Engage, Assess, Intervene, and Evaluate with Individuals, Families, Groups, Organizations and Communities							
a. Substantively and affectively prepare for action with individuals, families, groups, organizations, and communities							
b. Use empathy and other interpersonal skills							
c. Develop a mutually agreed-on focus of work and desired outcomes							
d. Collect, organize, and interpret client data							
e. Assess client strengths and limitations							
f. Develop mutually agreed-on intervention goals and objectives							
g. Select appropriate intervention strategies							
h. Initiate actions to achieve organizational goals							
i. Implement prevention interventions that enhance client capacities							
j. Help clients resolve problems							
k. Negotiate, mediate, and advocate for clients							
l. Facilitate transitions and endings							
m. Critically analyze, monitor, and evaluate interventions							

Chapter 5

Client Rights and Professional Expertise

Exercise 1: Complete Confidentiality: Is It Real?

Focus Competencies/Practice Behaviors:

EP 2.1.2 Apply social work ethical principles to guide professional practice
d. Apply strategies of ethical reasoning to arrive at principled decisions

GOAL: *For social workers to consider who the client is in dilemmas that are conflicting.*

> Arlene Johnson, 18 years old and single, is nearly six months pregnant. Yesterday, she came to the Women's Counseling Center to request help in getting an abortion. At the time of the abortion procedure, the fetus was considered viable and was placed in the neonatal intensive care unit as a high-risk premature baby. Arlene was extremely upset when she learned that the "abortion" had resulted in a live infant. She refused to look at the baby or take care of it. Instead, she threatened to sue the doctor and the hospital if the infant survived despite her expressed wish for an abortion. Arlene asked Robin Osborn, the hospital social worker, to make sure that the baby not be given intensive care, but rather be left alone so that it would die quickly.

Step 1: According to the traditional definition, the organization that pays the social worker's salary would be considered the client. But is the Women's Counseling Center the client of the social worker? Is the doctor, Arlene, or the infant the client of the social worker? Nowadays, the traditional definition may be too narrow, because it was originally devised for clients of independent professional practitioners in private practice.

Step 2: Use the ERS and EPS strategies from Chapter 4 to help you in your decision making.

Step 3: Share your assessment with your classmates and be prepared to defend your decision.

Exercise 2: Conflicting Client Obligations

Focus Competencies/Practice Behaviors:

EP 2.1.2 Apply social work ethical principles to guide professional practice
d. Apply strategies of ethical reasoning to arrive at principled decisions

GOAL: *To understand the responsibilities of the social worker as an agent of social control versus an agent of caring.*

Mrs. Linden is a fifth-grade teacher in the Abraham Lincoln Elementary School. The school is located in a neighborhood into which a large number of Central American families have moved recently. Joan Ramirez is the social worker assigned to this school, and her caseload includes several children in Mrs. Linden's class. Yesterday, Mrs. Linden asked Joan for help in keeping her pupils quietly in their seats. She told Joan that never in her 20 years as a teacher has she had as much trouble as this year. She thought that her troubles were caused by the many children who do not speak English well. Surely Joan could advise her how to handle these children so that they would be quiet and stay in their seats.

Step 1: Remember, Joan Ramirez was approached by Mrs. Linden, but the students are already her clients. Decide who the client is utilizing the following questions: Is the problem with the students, Mrs. Linden, or the school setting? What should Joan do about the role conflict? To whom does she owe loyalty? The social worker is not at all sure that the problem is with the pupils; perhaps the teacher is the real problem. What is the ethical thing to do?

Step 2: Answer the questions above and select three students with opposing views to debate their positions.

Exercise 3: Issues with Court Social Workers

Focus Competencies/Practice Behaviors:

EP 2.1.1 Identify as a Professional Social Worker and Conduct Oneself Accordingly
a. Advocate for client access to the services of social work
c. Attend to professional roles and boundaries
d. Demonstrate professional demeanor in behavior, appearance, and communication

GOAL: *Social workers working in the legal system face many challenges in their role as a court social worker where the court is the client and the persons that they are representing are also their client. How do social workers balance the best interest of both?*

In the probation service, social workers regularly prepare reports for the court judge. The judge takes these reports into consideration when making a final disposition of the case. The ethical dilemma here is that the social worker has responsibilities both toward the alleged delinquent and toward the court. She is helper and judicial fact finder. The client/worker helping relationship started during the first contact with the offender, long before the social worker has completed her evaluative assessment or presented her report to the judge.

Step 1: Divide into two groups.

Step 2: To whom does the social worker owe priority consideration—to the detainee or to the judge?

34

Step 3: Who is her client? Why did you choose that specific client?

Step 4: Bring the two groups together to discuss the reasons for their decisions.

Exercise 4: Professional Expertise and Self Determination

Focus Competencies/Practice Behaviors:

EP 2.1.3 Apply Critical Thinking to Inform and Communicate Professional Judgments
a. Distinguish, appraise, and integrate multiple sources of knowledge, including research based knowledge, and practice wisdom
b. Analyze models of assessment, prevention, intervention, and evaluations

GOAL: *This exercise is designed for social workers to consider how their knowledge affects decisions that they make with clients who are less knowledgeable about certain outcomes of decisions.*

Eleanor Pomer is 8 years old, the youngest of six siblings. She has been diagnosed with Down syndrome. For the last three years she has been a resident in a special school. According to her cottage parents, psychologist, teacher, and social worker, she functions on a moderate level but needs assistance with certain daily activities. Both of Eleanor's parents are employed. They rent the downstairs apartment of a two-family home in a working-class neighborhood about one hour's drive from Eleanor's school. For the past year, the Pomers have visited Eleanor once a month, and Eleanor has successfully spent one weekend a month at home. Both Eleanor and her family look forward to these visits. The school's staff feels that Eleanor now is ready to leave the school and live at home. The social worker has acquainted Eleanor's parents with this staff assessment. She has told them about the community resources that are available in their city and has urged them to take Eleanor home. However, the Pomers disagree with the staff recommendation. They are satisfied with the present arrangement because they feel that it would be too much of a strain on their other children if Eleanor again lived at home. The social worker is convinced that it would be best for Eleanor to leave the school and resume a more normal home life. She is aware that Eleanor is excited about the possibility of living with her parents and brothers and sisters.

Step 1: Using the ERS (figure 4.2) and EPS (figure 4.2) in Chapter 4 answer the following questions about the above scenario:

1. How much weight must the social worker give to the Pomers' and to Eleanor's wishes?
2. Should the most important criterion in reaching a decision be what is best for Eleanor?
3. Who decides what is best for Eleanor? What about the welfare of the other Pomer children? Does the social worker have an ethical right to manipulate the environment (e.g., by raising the tuition fee) in order to "help" the Pomers reach the decision that staff thinks is best for Eleanor? Are there standards in the Code that will help her decide what the correct decision is?

35

Step 2: For a grade, write your answers and show how you used the Assessments to come to your conclusions.

Exercise 5: Unclear Choices

Focus Competencies/Practice Behaviors:

EP 2.1.2 Apply social work ethical principles to guide professional practice
d. Apply strategies of ethical reasoning to arrive at principled decisions

GOAL: *This exercise is designed to help students begin to understand dilemmas from a client and societal perspective, the outcomes of which will be based on the social worker's values and decision making process.*

> Social worker Maria Espinosa has been working for one month with Allison Bode, an extremely thin, almost gaunt, reserved 17-year-old college freshman. Allison was referred to the Family Counseling Center by her pastor after she told him of her loneliness and obsessive thoughts. She came for help with the agreement and support of her parents. Allison is doing passing work academically but has been unsuccessful making friends at school, and for five months she has had practically no social life. This afternoon, Allison told Maria that her menstrual cycle has stopped. When Maria explored the situation, she learned that Allison is on an extremely restricted diet and exercises two to three hours a day to lose weight. She is slightly depressed but still able to concentrate on her schoolwork and reports she is seldom irritable. Based on all of this information, Maria is quite certain that Allison has anorexia and suggests she go to the college health service to consult with a physician. As soon as Allison heard the suggestion, she rejected it.

Step 1: Use ERS (figure 4.2) and EPS (figure 4.3) from your text and begin to rank order the principles from the most important to the least important. Use the following questions to guide your decision making process:

1. Is anorexia a case of clear and present danger that requires immediate action?
2. What harm would be done if a few more weekly sessions are used to help Allison act to protect her health and her visit to a physician is delayed?
3. Should Maria contact Allison's parents? Or should Maria call on the authority of the college and medical personnel to coerce Allison to attend to her illness? What is the ethically correct choice?

Role-Play

Exercise A: Ethical Conduct in a Tragic Situation

Focus Competencies/Practice Behaviors:

EP 2.1.2 Apply social work ethical principles to guide professional practice
a. Recognize and manage personal values in a way that allows professional values to guide practice
d. Apply strategies of ethical reasoning to arrive at principled decisions

GOAL: A basic ethical dilemma in social work practice arises out of two professional principles—at times contradictory—that all social workers have accepted: (1) the principle to provide professional help when needed or requested by a client in order to assure or improve that person's welfare, and (2) the principle to not interfere with a person's freedom. Ideally, a social worker should not experience any conflict between these two rights (or principles), but what if a person's wellbeing can be achieved only at the expense of his or her freedom? Who defines well-being? Who defines the need for professional help? Who can legitimately request professional help for another person?

Step 1: The scenario involves you as mitigation specialists for a Federal Public Defender's Office. Your job as a social worker in this capacity is to investigate mental health issues that are mitigating factors in Capital murder cases in which the client has been found guilty and is serving a sentence on death row. In this particular case the client wants to volunteer to be put to death and want no further appeals. You feel strongly that the client is not competent to make this decision, but understand his reasons for his decisions.

Step 3: Divide into groups of two. One person will be the social worker (mitigation specialists) and the other the inmate who wants to volunteer to die.

Step 4: After role playing the scenario discuss the questions located under the Goal section of this exercise.

37

Name: _____ **Date:** _____

Supervisor's Name: _____

Focus Competencies/Practice Behaviors:

EP 2.1.1 Identify as a Professional Social Worker and Conduct Oneself Accordingly
a. Advocate for client access to the services of social work
c. Attend to professional roles and boundaries
d. Demonstrate professional demeanor in behavior, appearance, and communication

EP 2.1.2 Apply social work ethical principles to guide professional practice
a. Recognize and manage personal values in a way that allows professional values to guide practice
d. Apply strategies of ethical reasoning to arrive at principled decisions

EP 2.1.3 Apply Critical Thinking to Inform and Communicate Professional Judgments
a. Distinguish, appraise, and integrate multiple sources of knowledge, including research based knowledge, and practice wisdom
b. Analyze models of assessment, prevention, intervention, and evaluations

Instructions:

A. Evaluate your work or your partner's work in the Focus Competencies/Practice Behaviors by completing the Competencies/Practice Behaviors Assessment form below
B. What other Competencies/Practice Behaviors did you use to complete these Exercises? Be sure to record them in your assessments

1.	I have attained this competency/practice behavior (in the range of 81 to 100%)
2.	I have largely attained this competency/practice behavior (in the range of 61 to 80%)
3.	I have partially attained this competency/practice behavior (in the range of 41 to 60%)
4.	I have made a little progress in attaining this competency/practice behavior (in the range of 21 to 40%)
5.	I have made almost no progress in attaining this competency/practice behavior (in the range of 0 to 20%)

Student and Evaluator Assessment Scale and Comments	0	1	2	3	4	5	Agree/Disagree/Comments
EP 2.1.1 Identify as a Professional Social Worker and Conduct Oneself Accordingly							
a. Advocate for client access to the services of social work							
b. Practice personal reflection and self-correction to assure continual professional development							

c.	Attend to professional roles and boundaries					
d.	Demonstrate professional demeanor in behavior, appearance, and communication					
e.	Engage in career-long learning					
f.	Use supervision and consultation					
EP 2.1.2 Apply Social Work Ethical Principles to Guide Professional Practice						
a.	Recognize and manage personal values in a way that allows professional values to guide practice					
b.	Make ethical decisions by applying NASW Code of Ethics and, as applicable, of the IFSW/IASSW Ethics in Social Work, Statement of Principles					
c.	Tolerate ambiguity in resolving ethical conflicts					
d.	Apply strategies of ethical reasoning to arrive at principled decisions					

EP 2.1.3 Apply Critical Thinking to Inform and Communicate Professional Judgments						
a.	Distinguish, appraise, and integrate multiple sources of knowledge, including research-based knowledge and practice wisdom					
b.	Analyze models of assessment, prevention, intervention, and evaluation					
c.	Demonstrate effective oral and written communication in working with individuals, families, groups, organizations, communities, and colleagues					
EP 2.1.4 Engage Diversity and Difference in Practice						
a.	Recognize the extent to which a culture's structures and values may oppress, marginalize, alienate, or create or enhance privilege and power					
b.	Gain sufficient self-awareness to eliminate the influence of personal biases and values in working with diverse groups					
c.	Recognize and communicate their understanding of the importance of difference in shaping life experiences					
d.	View themselves as learners and engage those with whom they work as informants					
EP 2.1.5 Advance Human Rights and Social and Economic Justice						
a.	Understand forms and mechanisms of oppression and discrimination					
b.	Advocate for human rights and social and economic justice					
c.	Engage in practices that advance social and economic justice					
EP 2.1.6 Engage in Research-Informed Practice and Practice-Informed Research						
a.	Use practice experience to inform scientific inquiry					
b.	Use research evidence to inform practice					

EP 2.1.7 Apply Knowledge of Human Behavior and the Social Environment							
a.	Utilize conceptual frameworks to guide the processes of assessment, intervention, and evaluation						
b.	Critique and apply knowledge to understand person and environment						
EP 2.1.8 Engage in Policy Practice to Advance Social and Economic Well-Being and to Deliver Effective Social Work Services							
a.	Analyze, formulate, and advocate for policies that advance social well-being						
b.	Collaborate with colleagues and clients for effective policy action						
EP 2.1.9 Respond to Contexts that Shape Practice							
a.	Continuously discover, appraise, and attend to changing locales, populations, scientific and technological developments, and emerging societal trends to provide relevant services						
b.	Provide leadership in promoting sustainable changes in service delivery and practice to improve the quality of social services						
EP 2.1.10 Engage, Assess, Intervene, and Evaluate with Individuals, Families, Groups, Organizations and Communities							
a.	Substantively and affectively prepare for action with individuals, families, groups, organizations, and communities						
b.	Use empathy and other interpersonal skills						
c.	Develop a mutually agreed-on focus of work and desired outcomes						
d.	Collect, organize, and interpret client data						
e.	Assess client strengths and limitations						
f.	Develop mutually agreed-on intervention goals and objectives						
g.	Select appropriate intervention strategies						
h.	Initiate actions to achieve organizational goals						
i.	Implement prevention interventions that enhance client capacities						
j.	Help clients resolve problems						
k.	Negotiate, mediate, and advocate for clients						
l.	Facilitate transitions and endings						
m.	Critically analyze, monitor, and evaluate interventions						

Chapter 6

Value Neutrality and Imposing Values

Exercise 1: Having a Baby and Substance Abuse

Focus Competencies/Practice Behaviors:

EP 2.1.2 Apply social work ethical principles to guide professional practice
d. Apply strategies of ethical reasoning to arrive at principled decisions

GOAL: *Social workers must, develop ways to deal with the value discrepancies that arise out of status difference between them and their clients.*

> Jeff Butz, a child protection services worker, received a call from the Community Hospital social worker. Mona Koss, a single mother with a substance abuse problem, gave birth to a baby girl two days ago. Mother and baby are due to be discharged tomorrow, but the hospital social worker does not think that the infant will be safe if she goes home with her mother. Mona, who has no permanent home, is currently living with a drug dealer who in the past has been involved in physical and sexual abuse situations.

Step 1: Write a report on the following:

1. Identify the differences and how they might affect both client and worker.
2. If possible, identify the problem in ways that avoid the conflicting values.
3. During the intake/assessment/diagnostic stage, the social worker should determine what may be the relationship between these value differences and the presenting problem.
4. Work first on parts of the problem that do not present value differences.
5. The social worker should discuss her findings with the clients so that together they can participate in determining whether these differences might complicate the social work process. No prior assumption should be made that a client is not ready and able to participate in such joint decision making.
6. A joint decision should be made whether to continue the social work process or whether the gap is so vast that it is preferable to continue the social work process with another social worker with more congruent values, if such a worker is available.

Exercise 2: Is Value Neutrality Real?

Focus Competencies/Practice Behaviors:

EP 2.1.2 Apply social work ethical principles to guide professional practice
d. Apply strategies of ethical reasoning to arrive at principled decisions

<u>GOAL</u>: *Social workers recognize the inevitability of values intruding into professional relationships and suggests that greater openness about this is correct and effective in achieving client goals.*

> Bess and Todd Moore have agreed to seek help to rescue their marriage. Bess recently discovered that Todd has been having sex with several other women over the past few years. Todd has told the social worker that his sexual relations with other women are merely physical. He has greater sexual needs than Bess and therefore cannot give up these relations. Yet he loves his wife and wants to continue this marriage. Bess is ready to forgive the past, but cannot bring herself to live with Todd knowing that he will continue to have sex with other women.

Step 1: Should the social worker keep her values to herself so that she will not influence the couple's decision? Should the social worker state her own values and then let Bess and Todd work on a solution to their problem? Which is the more ethical approach? Why?

Step 2: Answer the questions above and select three students with opposing views to debate their positions.

Exercise 3: Loyalty to Self or Family

<u>Focus Competencies/Practice Behaviors</u>:

E.P. 2.1.2 Apply social work ethical principles to guide professional practice
d. Apply strategies of ethical reasoning to arrive at principled decisions

<u>GOAL</u>: *Social workers working in the legal system face many challenges in their role as a court social worker where the court is the client and the persons that they are representing are also their client. How do social workers balance the best interest of both?*

> Rosa Arriga, a social worker at a family service agency, has seen Adira Salima for three sessions. Adira has been depressed, has experienced much conflict at home with her parents and other relatives, and has been subject to much anxiety on her job, where she works as a packer for minimum wage. All family members, including Adira, are recent immigrants to the United States. All must work because without everyone's paycheck they will not be able to maintain even a marginal existence. Her supervisor, who likes her, referred her to the agency for help. Adira told Rosa that her family continues to maintain the traditional culture of their country of origin. Thus, her parents will not allow her to have a normal U.S. social life because they are planning to arrange a marriage for her. She is not allowed to date. She cannot leave her family home because her earnings are insufficient to support herself elsewhere. Her knowledge of English and her other skills are not sufficient to qualify her for a better job. Adira vacillates between feeling pride at doing what is expected in her family's culture and wanting to become more Americanized by dating and deciding for herself whom she should marry.

42

Step 1: Write a report on the following questions and support your position:

1. What should be Rosa's approach?
2. Should she support Adira's loyalty to her family, knowing that they are all dependent on each other and that they are her only relatives in the United States?
3. Should she support Adira's struggle toward more independence?
4. If Adira has the possibility of living with extended family members or friends, should she be encouraged to leave home and live with them?
5. How should Rosa, who is a feminist, respond to this situation?
6. Would it be possible or appropriate for her to be value neutral when discussing options with Adira?
7. Would it make a difference if Rosa were from the same culture as Adira's family and a member of their community?

Exercise 4: Difference of Opinion

Focus Competencies/Practice Behaviors:

EP 2.1.3 Apply Critical Thinking to Inform and Communicate Professional Judgments
a. Distinguish, appraise, and integrate multiple sources of knowledge, including research based knowledge, and practice wisdom
b. Analyze models of assessment, prevention, intervention, and evaluations

GOAL: *This exercise is designed for social workers to consider how they feel about having different ideologies from the NASW Code of Ethics.*

> You are a social worker in a private practice. A male client has been referred to you who is married to a female, but continues to want to have affairs with other males. His wife is aware of this and is considering a divorce. However, both parties would like to try to work through their difficulties. You do not believe in extra-marital affairs and moreover you believe that homosexuality is sinful. You understand that the NASW Code of Ethics promotes self determination and being holding to a non-judgmental value base with regard to diversity.

Step 1: Knowing that your value base is opposite of the NASW Code of Ethics, should you continue in your practice if you continue to be assigned clients with these types of problems?

Step 2: Make sure that you have good information to support your position! After everyone has written their answers, divide the class into two sections…those who believe that they should remain in practice and those who do not.

Step 3: Organize a debate around these two ideologies.

Exercise 5: Conveying Values

Focus Competencies/Practice Behaviors:

2.1.3 Apply Critical Thinking to Inform and Communicate Professional Judgments
a. Distinguish, appraise, and integrate multiple sources of knowledge, including research based knowledge, and practice wisdom
b. Analyze models of assessment, prevention, intervention, and evaluations

GOAL: *This exercise is designed to help social work students begin to understand how their thoughts and actions convey their values.*

> You are a social worker in a public health clinic working with IV drug users who most of which have conveyed to you that they are sexually active. Yesterday during a heated discussion with one of your HIV positive sexually active clients you compared the risk of acquiring HIV from sexual activities with the risk of a fatal automobile accident. Your client seemed offended by your statement and asked why you chose to work in the public health center with that kind of attitude.

Step 1: If someone uses this comparison, does he or she communicate a value, or is this an example of value neutrality?

Step 2: Defend your answer with other members of the class.

Role-Play

Exercise A: Difficult Situations with Clients

Focus Competencies/Practice Behaviors:

EP 2.1.2 Apply social work ethical principles to guide professional practice
a. Recognize and manage personal values in a way that allows professional values to guide practice
d. Apply strategies of ethical reasoning to arrive at principled decisions

GOAL: *Your client feels very guilty about engaging in certain behavior. He asks your help, but he does not specify whether he wants help in dealing with his guilt or in extinguishing the behavior. Discuss the ethical implications of choosing either approach. Will the specific behavior make a difference in your ethical assessment?*

Step 1: Think about the above questions prior to your role play.

Step 2: You are working with a 15 year old juvenile sex offender who is in denial about raping a 4 year old girl.

Step 3: One student will play the social worker and the other the 15 year old juvenile.

44

Chapter 6

Competencies/Practice Behaviors Exercises Assessment:

Name: _____ **Date:** _____

Supervisor's Name: _____

Focus Competencies/Practice Behaviors:

EP 2.1.2 Apply social work ethical principles to guide professional practice
a. Recognize and manage personal values in a way that allows professional values to guide practice
d. Apply strategies of ethical reasoning to arrive at principled decisions

EP 2.1.3 Apply Critical Thinking to Inform and Communicate Professional Judgments
a. Distinguish, appraise, and integrate multiple sources of knowledge, including   research based knowledge, and practice wisdom
b. Analyze models of assessment, prevention, intervention, and evaluations

Instructions:

A.   Evaluate your work or your partner's work in the Focus Competencies/Practice Behaviors by completing the Competencies/Practice Behaviors Assessment form below
B.   What other Competencies/Practice Behaviors did you use to complete these Exercises? Be sure to record them in your assessments

1.	I have attained this competency/practice behavior (in the range of 81 to 100%)
2.	I have largely attained this competency/practice behavior (in the range of 61 to 80%)
3.	I have partially attained this competency/practice behavior (in the range of 41 to 60%)
4.	I have made a little progress in attaining this competency/practice behavior (in the range of 21 to 40%)
5.	I have made almost no progress in attaining this competency/practice behavior (in the range of 0 to 20%)

Student and Evaluator Assessment Scale and Comments	0	1	2	3	4	5	Agree/Disagree/Comments
EP 2.1.1 Identify as a Professional Social Worker and Conduct Oneself Accordingly							
a. Advocate for client access to the services of social work							
b. Practice personal reflection and self-correction to assure continual professional development							
c. Attend to professional roles and boundaries							
d. Demonstrate professional demeanor in behavior, appearance, and communication							
e. Engage in career-long learning							
f. Use supervision and consultation							

EP 2.1.2 Apply Social Work Ethical Principles to Guide Professional Practice							
a.	Recognize and manage personal values in a way that allows professional values to guide practice						
b.	Make ethical decisions by applying NASW Code of Ethics and, as applicable, of the IFSW/IASSW Ethics in Social Work, Statement of Principles						
c.	Tolerate ambiguity in resolving ethical conflicts						
d.	Apply strategies of ethical reasoning to arrive at principled decisions						

EP 2.1.3 Apply Critical Thinking to Inform and Communicate Professional Judgments							
a.	Distinguish, appraise, and integrate multiple sources of knowledge, including research-based knowledge and practice wisdom						
b.	Analyze models of assessment, prevention, intervention, and evaluation						
c.	Demonstrate effective oral and written communication in working with individuals, families, groups, organizations, communities, and colleagues						
EP 2.1.4 Engage Diversity and Difference in Practice							
a.	Recognize the extent to which a culture's structures and values may oppress, marginalize, alienate, or create or enhance privilege and power						
b.	Gain sufficient self-awareness to eliminate the influence of personal biases and values in working with diverse groups						
c.	Recognize and communicate their understanding of the importance of difference in shaping life experiences						
d.	View themselves as learners and engage those with whom they work as informants						
EP 2.1.5 Advance Human Rights and Social and Economic Justice							
a.	Understand forms and mechanisms of oppression and discrimination						
b.	Advocate for human rights and social and economic justice						
c.	Engage in practices that advance social and economic justice						
EP 2.1.6 Engage in Research-Informed Practice and Practice-Informed Research							
a.	Use practice experience to inform scientific inquiry						
b.	Use research evidence to inform practice						

EP 2.1.7 Apply Knowledge of Human Behavior and the Social Environment							
a. Utilize conceptual frameworks to guide the processes of assessment, intervention, and evaluation							
b. Critique and apply knowledge to understand person and environment							
EP 2.1.8 Engage in Policy Practice to Advance Social and Economic Well-Being and to Deliver Effective Social Work Services							
a. Analyze, formulate, and advocate for policies that advance social well-being							
b. Collaborate with colleagues and clients for effective policy action							
EP 2.1.9 Respond to Contexts that Shape Practice							
a. Continuously discover, appraise, and attend to changing locales, populations, scientific and technological developments, and emerging societal trends to provide relevant services							
b. Provide leadership in promoting sustainable changes in service delivery and practice to improve the quality of social services							
EP 2.1.10 Engage, Assess, Intervene, and Evaluate with Individuals, Families, Groups, Organizations and Communities							
a. Substantively and affectively prepare for action with individuals, families, groups, organizations, and communities							
b. Use empathy and other interpersonal skills							
c. Develop a mutually agreed-on focus of work and desired outcomes							
d. Collect, organize, and interpret client data							
e. Assess client strengths and limitations							
f. Develop mutually agreed-on intervention goals and objectives							
g. Select appropriate intervention strategies							
h. Initiate actions to achieve organizational goals							
i. Implement prevention interventions that enhance client capacities							
j. Help clients resolve problems							
k. Negotiate, mediate, and advocate for clients							
l. Facilitate transitions and endings							
m. Critically analyze, monitor, and evaluate interventions							

Chapter 7

The Professional Relationship: Limits, Dilemmas, and Problems

Exercise 1: Treatment of an Inferiority Complex

Focus Competencies/Practice Behaviors:

EP 2.1.2 Apply social work ethical principles to guide professional practice
d. Apply strategies of ethical reasoning to arrive at principled decisions

GOAL: *For social workers to understand that sexual intimacy between professional social workers and clients is not simply an ethical breach. Such intimacy with clients is also grounds for legal action in all*
50 states,

> Jill Jordan, a 35-year-old divorcee, has been a client of the Family Consultation Center for a number of months. Her presenting problem is that she feels inadequate, unattractive, and stymied in her career. She feels that her negative self-image contributed to her divorce and has become a barrier to advancement on the job. Finding fulfillment in her career and developing more rewarding relationships depend on her becoming more positive about herself and being more optimistic. Bob Temple, an experienced social worker, was assigned as her therapist. A contract was established with the presenting problem as the focus. During the course of treatment, Bob was very understanding and warmly responsive to Jill. His objective was to restore Jill's faith in herself. As treatment proceeded, Jill did not hesitate to express her admiration of Bob. At the end of one session, she spontaneously hugged him and said how appreciative she was for all his help. As she experienced more successes in her life, she would ask for a hug as a sign of his support for her. Still later, she made it evident that she was attracted to Bob and would not reject his interest in her. Bob was also attracted to Jill. He wanted to pursue a personal relationship with her, but he knew that the professional ethics demanded that he not do so. How should Bob handle this issue?

Step 1: Review questions 1-7 on pages 131 and 132 from your text.

Step 2: Divide into two groups. Your groups should narrow the list to three choices

Step 3: Have each group decide on one of their chosen answers and have the two groups debate their answers providing solid reasoning for their choices.

Exercise 2: Is Honesty the Best Policy?

Focus Competencies/Practice Behaviors:

EP 2.1.2 Apply social work ethical principles to guide professional practice
d. Apply strategies of ethical reasoning to arrive at principled decisions

GOAL: *To assist social workers in problem solving issues that require responses that may or may not be truthful.*

Gail Silva is a single parent raising two daughters, ages 6 and 7. She has been trying to find a part-time job to supplement her meager child support income ever since her younger daughter started kindergarten two years ago. She has been repeatedly refused a job because she has had no prior work experience. By now she has become very frustrated and has developed a very negative self-image. She believes that nobody wants her—neither as a spouse nor as a worker. This morning, she told you excitedly that she thinks she has found a job. As she describes the job, you realize that she is telling you about an employer who is known to exploit his workers and who pays below the minimum wage, when he pays at all. Should you tell Gail the truth about her prospective employer? Or should you share her enthusiasm, hoping that things will work out? What is the ethical thing to do?

Step 1: Consider the following options:

• Don't say anything.
• Tell her everything and urge her not to take this job.
• Point out the advantages (a job, an employment history) and disadvantages (low pay, exploitation) and let her make the decision.

Step 2: Which option would you choose and why?

Step 3: For extra credit write a one page paper explaining your choice and why you chose it.

Exercise 3: Can Deception be Justified?

Focus Competencies/Practice Behaviors:

EP 2.1.2 Apply social work ethical principles to guide professional practice
d. Apply strategies of ethical reasoning to arrive at principled decisions

GOAL: *To exam the ethical implications for a social worker who lies*

Art Elder, age 34, is a high school teacher. At present he is a patient at University Hospital because he has a growth on his foot. His physician told him that there are two ways of treating this problem. Both involve some risks. When Art asked what he would advise, the physician suggested surgery. Sally Brown is the social worker in the surgical department. From her discussion with the resident, she learned that Dr. Kutner, the physician, did not tell the patient all the available choices and that he withheld information about the option with the least risk Evidently, he weighted his presentation in favor of the experimental surgical treatment method that he is just now developing.

Step 1: Divide into two groups.

Step 2: From the following list decide if any of the reasons justify deceiving the client or telling less than the truth:
• To make a client-selected goal less desirable
• To create new goals
• To obscure options
• To increase options
• To change the cost/benefit estimate for one or more options
• To increase or decrease client uncertainty
• To increase or decrease client anxiety
• To protect the client from a "damaging" truth
• To protect the effectiveness of the current intervention strategy
• To obtain the client's "informed" consent
• To protect confidential information received from a third party
• To strengthen the relationship with a client by lying at his request to a third party
• To increase the worker's power over a client by withholding information
• To make the worker look good by papering over mistakes she has made

Step 3: Discuss your choice(s) during a classroom discussion.

Exercise 4: The Choice between Loyalty to a Colleague or to a Practical Cause

Focus Competencies/Practice Behaviors:

EP 2.1.2 Apply social work ethical principles to guide professional practice
d. Apply strategies of ethical reasoning to arrive at principled decisions

GOAL: *This exercise is designed to help social workers think about how to handle situations where there are two viable but conflicting issues.*

The Frans family contributed a considerable sum of money to the Uptown Community Center to furnish and equip a music appreciation room in memory of their mother. An appropriate plaque marks the room. Since the center accepted the contribution, the neighborhood has experienced a large influx of immigrants from Southeast Asia. Because of their needs, the room is now used for purposes other than those designated by the donors. You are the center's associate director. You know how important the music appreciation room is to the family. There is a good possibility of obtaining additional donations for other projects from this family, but if the family discovers that their room is no longer used for music appreciation activities, they may lose interest in the Uptown Community Center. At the monthly meeting of the board of directors, you meet Gerald Frans. He asks you how the music appreciation room is doing.

Step 1: Divide into dyads. Using the ERS (figure 4.2) and EPS (figure 4.2) in Chapter 4 answer the following questions about the above scenario:

How should you reply? Do you tell the truth? Do you try to avoid the issue by shifting the conversation to another area? Do you tell a little untruth, such as "the immigrants love music"? Or not? What is the ethically correct response? How do you decide?

Step 2: For a grade, write your answers and show how you used the Assessments to come to your conclusions.

Step 3: Discuss your answers with the rest of the class.

Exercise 5: Ethical Issues with Billing

Focus Competencies/Practice Behaviors:

EP 2.1.2 Apply social work ethical principles to guide professional practice
d. Apply strategies of ethical reasoning to arrive at principled decisions

GOAL: *This exercise is designed to help students begin to understand that they will face with regard to the practicality of conducting social work as a business.*

> Christine Sales is seeing a private practice social worker. At their initial session last week, she mentioned that she hoped her insurance company would reimburse her for these sessions. Today, Christine brought in the insurance forms and asked her social worker to complete them. The social worker, who was familiar with the requirements of this insurance company, realized right away that she would have to report a more "serious" diagnosis than was clinically indicated if she were to qualify the client for reimbursement.

Step 1: Review your text from the bottom of page 139 to the top of page 140.

Step 2: Discuss your views as a class.

<u>**Role-Play**</u>

Exercise A: Can Vicarious Trauma and Stress Affect Social Work Practice?
Focus Competencies/Practice Behaviors:

EP 2.1.2 Apply social work ethical principles to guide professional practice
a. Recognize and manage personal values in a way that allows professional values to guide practice
d. Apply strategies of ethical reasoning to arrive at principled decisions

<u>GOAL:</u> *Although it is unclear whether work with clients who have experienced trauma is directly related to compassion fatigue, vicarious trauma, or secondary traumatic stress, it is clear that social workers are at risk for these conditions, which impact their ability to work with clients.*

Step 1: The scenario involves Allison Webster i a social worker who has been working in Haiti since a few months after the earthquake on January 12, 2010. Allison is single, recently completed her MSW, and loves to travel, so she was very excited when she was offered a position working in Port-au-Prince. It has now been over a year since she arrived in Haiti,
and she is working with families who lost everything in the earthquake and are still struggling to put their lives back together. Every client she sees has vivid memories of the earthquake and many of them want to share their experience. Recently, thoughts of her clients' stories have been intruding on Allison's thoughts and dreams, and she feels as if she will scream if she hears one more earthquake story. Allison knows that her work is important, but lately she is wondering if she is really cut out to be a social worker because she often feels impatient and unsympathetic with her clients. Mattie James and Allison belong to the same social work support group and as they discuss issues of their work, Mattie begins to wonder if Allison is experiencing compassion fatigue, vicarious trauma, or secondary traumatic stress.

Step 1: Divide into dyads. One student will role play Mattie and the other Allison.

Step 2: Allison should keep in mind all of the issues involved in her life during the role play.

Step 3: Mattie should consider the following questions during her interactions with Allison:
What are the ethical dilemmas in this situation?
How should Mattie respond to Allison's request for help?
Can (or should) Mattie diagnose Allison's problem based on the support group discussion?
If Mattie suspects that Allison can no longer effectively and ethically provide social work services to her clients, does Mattie have a responsibility to report her suspicions to the agency that employs Allison?

Chapter 7

Competencies/Practice Behaviors Exercises Assessment:

Name: _____ **Date:** _____

Supervisor's Name: _____

Focus Competencies/Practice Behaviors:

EP 2.1.2 Apply social work ethical principles to guide professional practice
a. Recognize and manage personal values in a way that allows professional values to guide practice
d. Apply strategies of ethical reasoning to arrive at principled decisions

Instructions:

A. Evaluate your work or your partner's work in the Focus Competencies/Practice Behaviors by completing the Competencies/Practice Behaviors Assessment form below
B. What other Competencies/Practice Behaviors did you use to complete these Exercises? Be sure to record them in your assessments

1.	I have attained this competency/practice behavior (in the range of 81 to 100%)
2.	I have largely attained this competency/practice behavior (in the range of 61 to 80%)
3.	I have partially attained this competency/practice behavior (in the range of 41 to 60%)
4.	I have made a little progress in attaining this competency/practice behavior (in the range of 21 to 40%)
5.	I have made almost no progress in attaining this competency/practice behavior (in the range of 0 to 20%)

Student and Evaluator Assessment Scale and Comments	0	1	2	3	4	5	Agree/Disagree/Comments
EP 2.1.1 Identify as a Professional Social Worker and Conduct Oneself Accordingly							
a. Advocate for client access to the services of social work							
b. Practice personal reflection and self-correction to assure continual professional development							
c. Attend to professional roles and boundaries							
d. Demonstrate professional demeanor in behavior, appearance, and communication							
e. Engage in career-long learning							
f. Use supervision and consultation							
EP 2.1.2 Apply Social Work Ethical Principles to Guide Professional Practice							
a. Recognize and manage personal values in a way that allows professional values to guide practice							

53

b.	Make ethical decisions by applying NASW Code of Ethics and, as applicable, of the IFSW/IASSW Ethics in Social Work, Statement of Principles						
c.	Tolerate ambiguity in resolving ethical conflicts						
d.	Apply strategies of ethical reasoning to arrive at principled decisions						

EP 2.1.3 Apply Critical Thinking to Inform and Communicate Professional Judgments							
a.	Distinguish, appraise, and integrate multiple sources of knowledge, including research-based knowledge and practice wisdom						
b.	Analyze models of assessment, prevention, intervention, and evaluation						
c.	Demonstrate effective oral and written communication in working with individuals, families, groups, organizations, communities, and colleagues						
EP 2.1.4 Engage Diversity and Difference in Practice							
a.	Recognize the extent to which a culture's structures and values may oppress, marginalize, alienate, or create or enhance privilege and power						
b.	Gain sufficient self-awareness to eliminate the influence of personal biases and values in working with diverse groups						
c.	Recognize and communicate their understanding of the importance of difference in shaping life experiences						
d.	View themselves as learners and engage those with whom they work as informants						
EP 2.1.5 Advance Human Rights and Social and Economic Justice							
a.	Understand forms and mechanisms of oppression and discrimination						
b.	Advocate for human rights and social and economic justice						
c.	Engage in practices that advance social and economic justice						
EP 2.1.6 Engage in Research-Informed Practice and Practice-Informed Research							
a.	Use practice experience to inform scientific inquiry						
b.	Use research evidence to inform practice						
EP 2.1.7 Apply Knowledge of Human Behavior and the Social Environment							
a.	Utilize conceptual frameworks to guide the processes of assessment, intervention, and evaluation						
b.	Critique and apply knowledge to understand person and environment						

EP 2.1.8 Engage in Policy Practice to Advance Social and Economic Well-Being and to Deliver Effective Social Work Services						
a.	Analyze, formulate, and advocate for policies that advance social well-being					
b.	Collaborate with colleagues and clients for effective policy action					
EP 2.1.9 Respond to Contexts that Shape Practice						
a.	Continuously discover, appraise, and attend to changing locales, populations, scientific and technological developments, and emerging societal trends to provide relevant services					
b.	Provide leadership in promoting sustainable changes in service delivery and practice to improve the quality of social services					
EP 2.1.10 Engage, Assess, Intervene, and Evaluate with Individuals, Families, Groups, Organizations and Communities						
a.	Substantively and affectively prepare for action with individuals, families, groups, organizations, and communities					
b.	Use empathy and other interpersonal skills					
c.	Develop a mutually agreed-on focus of work and desired outcomes					
d.	Collect, organize, and interpret client data					
e.	Assess client strengths and limitations					
f.	Develop mutually agreed-on intervention goals and objectives					
g.	Select appropriate intervention strategies					
h.	Initiate actions to achieve organizational goals					
i.	Implement prevention interventions that enhance client capacities					
j.	Help clients resolve problems					
k.	Negotiate, mediate, and advocate for clients					
l.	Facilitate transitions and endings					
m.	Critically analyze, monitor, and evaluate interventions					

Chapter 8

Confidentiality and Informed Consent

Exercise 1: Treatment of an Inferiority Complex

Focus Competencies/Practice Behaviors:

EP 2.1.3 Apply Critical Thinking to Inform and Communicate Professional Judgments
a. Distinguish, appraise, and integrate multiple sources of knowledge, including research based knowledge, and practice wisdom
b. Analyze models of assessment, prevention, intervention, and evaluations

GOAL: *For social workers to understand that it is incumbent on them to take measures to protect their clients.*

> A residential treatment center for severely emotionally disturbed clients has developed a method of involving their clients in physically challenging, adventurous events to heighten self-esteem and expand the children's repertoire of physical skills and problem solving. A newspaper reporter has asked to do a story about the events which will likely increase monitory donations to the facility. The center obtains general, cursory written permissions from the children's parents and guardians for the children to be observed in a range of circumstances at the facility. Once the story is printed two social workers observe that the children's families are depicted as dysfunctional, and the children are too young to understand the implications of being identifiable are described with intimate details of their lives and troubles. The story is nearly complete, the facility administrator believes it is a worthy project, and most of the staff is excited about the likely publicity. However, the staff social workers have concerns that the story may be exploitive of their clients. What should these social workers do?

Step 1: Review the NASW Code of Ethics with regard to informed consent.

Step 2: How can an amicable answer to this problem be obtained?

Exercise 2: To Whom Does the Social Worker Owe Necessary Loyalty?

Focus Competencies/Practice Behaviors:

EP 2.1.2 Apply social work ethical principles to guide professional practice
d. Apply strategies of ethical reasoning to arrive at principled decisions

GOAL: *To generate discussion and critical thinking about legal and ethical dilemmas.*

56

Social worker Jean Fisher is a marriage counselor and family therapist in the Old Town Family Consultation Center, a nonsectarian agency. Sue and Dean Kern have been coming to her for marital therapy once a week for the past two months. Though their problem is not critical, they came to seek help while their marriage was still salvageable. They have made good progress toward reaching their goal. During today's session, Dean mentioned that he has continued to receive supplemental security income (SSI) payments for his aged mother, who lived with them until she moved overseas two years ago. She now makes her home with his sister, who lives in England.

Step 1: Consult the NASW Code of Ethics

Step 2: Should Jean report this case as possible fraud? Does client/worker confidentiality cover this communication?

Step 3: Write down your findings and discuss them with your class.

Exercise 3: Can Deception be Justified?

Focus Competencies or Practice Behaviors:

 EP 2.1.2 Apply social work ethical principles to guide professional practice
d. Apply strategies of ethical reasoning to arrive at principled decisions

GOAL: *To exam situations where social workers are asked to share confidential information about relatives*

Debbie Roberts is a 12-year-old eighth-grader who is 10 weeks pregnant. She has been a good student, and her teacher reports that she has never had any problems with Debbie. The school nurse referred Debbie to the school social worker because Debbie refused to discuss her condition with the nurse. At first, Debbie also refused to speak to the social worker, but later she told her that she did not want to have an abortion. She repeatedly emphasized that she did not want her parents to know that she was pregnant. Debbie will not reveal who the father is, and the social worker suspects that Debbie may have been sexually abused.

Step 1: Answer the following questions:

1. Should Debbie's parents be told about their daughter's pregnancy?
2. Should the social worker know who father of the baby is before speaking to her parents?
3. Should child protective services be told about the situation?
4. What is the ethical approach to this ambiguous situation?

Exercise 4: Conflict Between the Right of the Client and Duty of the Social Worker

Focus Competencies/Practice Behaviors:

EP 2.1.2 Apply social work ethical principles to guide professional practice
d. Apply strategies of ethical reasoning to arrive at principled decisions

GOAL: *This exercise is designed to help social workers understand the need to use diplomacy and best practice skills to conduct themselves in an ethical manner with their clients and the agency.*

A social worker in a sectarian family agency, who had great differences with the agency regarding policy issues, resigned his position giving the appropriate notice. The agency immediately informed him that his employment was terminated and that he would be precluded from any further contact with clients. The social worker feels he is being prevented from terminating appropriately with his clients but knows that he would need to take confidential information about the clients if he were to decide to engage in terminating with his clients without the agency's consent.

Step 1: Divide into dyads. Using the ERS (figure 4.2) and EPS (figure 4.2) in Chapter 4 answer the following questions about the above scenario:

How can the social worker resolve this issue within the agency without risking legal action of taking confidential information home?

Does the social worker have an ethical obligation to help the organization carry out its services ethically?

Step 2: For a grade, write your answers and show how you used the Assessments to come to your conclusions.

Step 3: Discuss your answers with the rest of the class.

Exercise 5: Outreach for Archie

Focus Competencies/Practice Behaviors:

EP 2.1.2 Apply social work ethical principles to guide professional practice
d. Apply strategies of ethical reasoning to arrive at principled decisions

GOAL: *This exercise is designed to help social workers realize that the decision to intervene in a person's life must never be taken lightly. To limit a person's freedom by*

58

removing her from her home and placing her in an institution is a very serious decision, which ordinarily should not be made without the person's consent.

Muriel Palmieri is an outreach worker for the Downtown Elderly Program (DEP). She has organized a group of volunteers who regularly visit with homebound older people. These volunteers have been trained to identify older people who need additional help so that they can report their names to the DEP. One of the volunteers recently told Muriel that she had discovered a bedridden older man in a cold and dirty fourth floor walk-up apartment. Archie Walker was probably not as old or as feeble as he appeared, but the volunteer thought that he required more care than the occasional help provided by his 79-year-old neighbor, who brought him food whenever he thought of it. When this neighbor forgot to come, as happened not infrequently, Archie subsisted for days on cold water and bread. It had been years since Archie last saw a doctor. He seemed delighted with the volunteer's visit and begged her to come again soon. Muriel told the volunteer that she would see what could be done to make Archie more comfortable. When Muriel visited Archie, he welcomed her warmly. She was able to confirm the volunteer's observations. Archie seemed relatively alert. Muriel thought that his dissatisfaction with his present condition was realistic and a hopeful sign, indicative of a capacity to participate in developing plans for the future. Archie explained that his only income came from Social Security. He had never heard of the federal Supplemental Security Income (SSI) program. Muriel suspected that he would qualify for SSI. Archie said that he could not afford to move to another apartment, but he insisted that he did not want to go to an "old folks' home." Muriel explained about many of the programs that were available to help persons in his situation. She listed the advantages and disadvantages of each and indicated the time it might take before each program or service would start for him. She also noted how she could help him qualify. Among the programs they discussed were SSI, Meals-on-Wheels, health visitors, homemakers, Title 8 housing, and the Manor Apartments. Archie seemed bewildered by the many programs from which he could choose and by the many decisions he had to make. He asked Muriel to do whatever was best for him.

Step 1: If you were in Murial's place what would you have done? Identify some of the ethical issues you might encounter if you were to try to help Archie.

Step 2: Discuss your views as a class.

Role-Play

Exercise A: Duty to Protect

Focus Competencies/Practice Behaviors:

EP 2.1.2 Apply social work ethical principles to guide professional practice
a. Recognize and manage personal values in a way that allows professional values to guide practice
d. Apply strategies of ethical reasoning to arrive at principled decisions

GOAL: *To be aware that in addition to varying state legislation and court decisions concerning the duty to protect, a fundamental issue of concern is the assessment of the probability of violence.*

Rufus Hall is seeking help with his four-year marriage. According to Rufus, his wife, Sara, refuses to come to counseling with him and has been threatening to get a divorce. Rufus reports that on occasion he gets very angry with his wife and has slapped her once or twice. During one session, he said that he loves his wife and would kill her if she goes through with her threat to get a divorce. His social worker, Jillian Adams, who lives in the same community as Rufus and Sara, knows that Sara recently saw a lawyer about a divorce. To date, Rufus has only spoken of slaps, but Jillian is uncertain how to respond to his comment that he would kill Sara if she divorces him.

Step 1: Divide into dyads. One student will role play Rufus and the other Jillian Adams.

Step 2: Rufus should keep in mind all of the issues involved in his life during the role play.

Step 3: Jillian should consider the following questions during her interactions with Rufus:

Should Jillian report the husband's comment as a threat? If yes, to whom?
How can she assess the seriousness of his statement?
Would it matter if she knew his "slaps" had been more violent than he reported?
What information would be helpful in deciding whether the threat to Sara's safety should be reported?

Name: _____ **Date:** _____

Supervisor's Name: _____

Focus Competencies/Practice Behaviors:

EP 2.1.2 Apply social work ethical principles to guide professional practice
d. Apply strategies of ethical reasoning to arrive at principled decisions

EP 2.1.3 Apply Critical Thinking to Inform and Communicate Professional Judgments
a. Distinguish, appraise, and integrate multiple sources of knowledge, including research based knowledge, and practice wisdom
b. Analyze models of assessment, prevention, intervention, and evaluations

Instructions:

A.   Evaluate your work or your partner's work in the Focus Competencies/Practice Behaviors by completing the Competencies/Practice Behaviors Assessment form below
B.   What other Competencies/Practice Behaviors did you use to complete these Exercises? Be sure to record them in your assessments

1.	I have attained this competency/practice behavior (in the range of 81 to 100%)
2.	I have largely attained this competency/practice behavior (in the range of 61 to 80%)
3.	I have partially attained this competency/practice behavior (in the range of 41 to 60%)
4.	I have made a little progress in attaining this competency/practice behavior (in the range of 21 to 40%)
5.	I have made almost no progress in attaining this competency/practice behavior (in the range of 0 to 20%)

Student and Evaluator Assessment Scale and Comments	0	1	2	3	4	5	Agree/Disagree/Comments
EP 2.1.1 Identify as a Professional Social Worker and Conduct Oneself Accordingly							
a. Advocate for client access to the services of social work							
b. Practice personal reflection and self-correction to assure continual professional development							
c. Attend to professional roles and boundaries							
d. Demonstrate professional demeanor in behavior, appearance, and communication							
e. Engage in career-long learning							
f. Use supervision and consultation							

EP 2.1.2 Apply Social Work Ethical Principles to Guide Professional Practice						
a. Recognize and manage personal values in a way that allows professional values to guide practice						
b. Make ethical decisions by applying NASW Code of Ethics and, as applicable, of the IFSW/IASSW Ethics in Social Work, Statement of Principles						
c. Tolerate ambiguity in resolving ethical conflicts						
d. Apply strategies of ethical reasoning to arrive at principled decisions						

EP 2.1.3 Apply Critical Thinking to Inform and Communicate Professional Judgments						
a. Distinguish, appraise, and integrate multiple sources of knowledge, including research-based knowledge and practice wisdom						
b. Analyze models of assessment, prevention, intervention, and evaluation						
c. Demonstrate effective oral and written communication in working with individuals, families, groups, organizations, communities, and colleagues						
EP 2.1.4 Engage Diversity and Difference in Practice						
a. Recognize the extent to which a culture's structures and values may oppress, marginalize, alienate, or create or enhance privilege and power						
b. Gain sufficient self-awareness to eliminate the influence of personal biases and values in working with diverse groups						
c. Recognize and communicate their understanding of the importance of difference in shaping life experiences						
d. View themselves as learners and engage those with whom they work as informants						
EP 2.1.5 Advance Human Rights and Social and Economic Justice						
a. Understand forms and mechanisms of oppression and discrimination						
b. Advocate for human rights and social and economic justice						
c. Engage in practices that advance social and economic justice						
EP 2.1.6 Engage in Research-Informed Practice and Practice-Informed Research						
a. Use practice experience to inform scientific inquiry						
b. Use research evidence to inform practice						
EP 2.1.7 Apply Knowledge of Human Behavior and the Social Environment						
a. Utilize conceptual frameworks to guide the processes of assessment, intervention, and evaluation						

b.	Critique and apply knowledge to understand person and environment					
EP 2.1.8 Engage in Policy Practice to Advance Social and Economic Well-Being and to Deliver Effective Social Work Services						
a.	Analyze, formulate, and advocate for policies that advance social well-being					
b.	Collaborate with colleagues and clients for effective policy action					
EP 2.1.9 Respond to Contexts that Shape Practice						
a.	Continuously discover, appraise, and attend to changing locales, populations, scientific and technological developments, and emerging societal trends to provide relevant services					
b.	Provide leadership in promoting sustainable changes in service delivery and practice to improve the quality of social services					
EP 2.1.10 Engage, Assess, Intervene, and Evaluate with Individuals, Families, Groups, Organizations and Communities						
a.	Substantively and affectively prepare for action with individuals, families, groups, organizations, and communities					
b.	Use empathy and other interpersonal skills					
c.	Develop a mutually agreed-on focus of work and desired outcomes					
d.	Collect, organize, and interpret client data					
e.	Assess client strengths and limitations					
f.	Develop mutually agreed-on intervention goals and objectives					
g.	Select appropriate intervention strategies					
h.	Initiate actions to achieve organizational goals					
i.	Implement prevention interventions that enhance client capacities					
j.	Help clients resolve problems					
k.	Negotiate, mediate, and advocate for clients					
l.	Facilitate transitions and endings					
m.	Critically analyze, monitor, and evaluate interventions					

Exercise 1: Limited Resources

<u>Focus Competencies/Practice Behaviors:</u>

EP 2.1.2 Apply social work ethical principles to guide professional practice
d. Apply strategies of ethical reasoning to arrive at principled decisions

<u>GOAL:</u> *For social workers to understand that it is incumbent on them to take measures to protect their clients.*

> Doreen's child is a 13-year-old with a history of school truancy, alcohol and drug experimentation, and several attempts at running away from home. Her parents appear warm and accepting, but the family agency worker who has been meeting with Doreen for the past four weeks suspects that the real problem is Doreen's home life. Today was the fifth session with Doreen. The conversation was routine, and little of significance was said until three minutes before the next client's scheduled appointment. Suddenly, Doreen said that both her father and older brother have tried repeatedly to have sex with her, but thus far she has not let them go all the way. When she told her mother about this, she was told to forget it had ever happened. As Doreen related this information, she became noticeably more upset. The social worker realized that this interview could not be terminated just because time was up. Doreen was agitated, and the session could not be ended at that point. Later, the worker would need to make a report of suspected child abuse to child protective services. She was not sure how long the discussion with Doreen would take and was worried about how long she could keep the next client waiting. Doreen could easily use all of the next client's hour, but that would not be fair to the other clients scheduled for that day, who may also be experiencing serious difficulties.

Step 1: How would you handle this situation?

Step 2: Divide into three groups. Each group will have a large piece of poster paper to write on. You will have 10 minutes to come up with an answer that is equitable to all parties using figures 4.2 and/or 4.3 to process this problem.

Step 3: Discuss your answers with one another.

Exercise 2: Unofficial Unequal Treatment

Focus Competencies/Practice Behaviors:

EP 2.1.2 Apply social work ethical principles to guide professional practice
d. Apply strategies of ethical reasoning to arrive at principled decisions

GOAL: *To generate discussion and critical thinking about legal and ethical dilemmas.*

Latoya Jefferson is a volunteer social worker in an emergency food pantry where persons come to obtain needed food for themselves and their families. The only requirement is that people answer several questions: name, household size, and source of income, not subject to verification. No one asks about living situations (a place to cook, ages of children, or special dietary needs). There is not enough paid staff and volunteers to run the pantry as it should be operated. Because of the shortage of supplies, families can only receive food once a month, but over time the staff and volunteers still get to know individuals and their situations. Latoya, the paid director of the pantry, recently discovered that Keisha Attlee, a volunteer social worker, favors some clients over others. She chooses favorites who are especially friendly or who have well-disciplined and cute children. She also identifies those she thinks abuse the system; when food is in short supply, she refers the "abusers" to another pantry while assisting her favorites. When Latoya questioned Keisha about her discriminating so that some get needed supplies while others are referred elsewhere, Keisha replied, "In my view I am giving food to those who are most needy and cooperative. Aren't they entitled to the help? I know they will make good use of the food. Those I refer elsewhere may be selling the food and buying beer and whiskey. Furthermore, as a volunteer I don't want to be supervised. If you keep bothering me, I will just leave and you can do the distribution yourself." How should Keisha's supervisor handle this situation?

Step 1: Consult the NASW Code of Ethics regarding discriminatory practices and consult your text regarding this scenario.

Step 2: Write a one page paper about the process you would use to remedy this issue.

Exercise 3: Can Deception be Justified?

Focus Competencies/Practice Behaviors:

EP 2.1.4 Engage Diversity and Difference in Practice
b. Gain sufficient self-awareness to eliminate the influence of personal biases and values in working with diverse groups.

GOAL: *To exam situations where social workers are asked to share confidential information about relatives*

65

A social worker employed in a county social services agency as an eligibility worker has learned that local welfare reforms direct that she report any new children born to current welfare recipients. She fears that this new reporting requirement could prevent children born into welfare families from receiving income supports later in their lives. The worker is aware of the requirement that social workers should comply with the law. However, she is convinced that reporting newborns might preclude future essential services. The social worker also believes that the new regulations will create a new class of citizens (children born to welfare mothers) that might be discriminated against in various ways. She feels caught between complying with the law and ignoring the law to prevent what she views as likely injustice.

Step 1: Consult the NASW Code of Ethics regarding conflict with agency policies or relevant laws or regulations.

Step2: Define the ethical issue(s)

Step 3: Give all possible solutions to the issue(s) at hand using the NASW Code of Ethics as a guide.

Exercise 4: Addressing Discriminatory Practice

Focus Competencies/Practice Behaviors:

EP 2.1.2 Apply social work ethical principles to guide professional practice
d. Apply strategies of ethical reasoning to arrive at principled decisions

GOAL: *This exercise is designed to help social workers understand the need to use evidence in all areas of practice.*

Janice McNally, a highly successful attorney with a very busy professional life, including frequent work-related travel, and Virginia Barker, a sales clerk in a mall who frequently changes jobs, have been in a long-term relationship. They agreed to have a child to be conceived by Janice as the biological mother. When Susan was born, Virginia began, but failed to complete, the adoption process. Both Janice and Virginia love the child and at first shared equally in the parenting. Janice's high income made possible many extras for Susan such as play groups, day camps, arts and crafts classes, and music lessons. For a number of years, the couple remained compatible and cared for Susan together, and the child bonded with both of them. When Susan was 8 years old, Virginia and Janice separated; Virginia asked for joint custody of Susan, which Janice refused to provide. Judge Watson assigned Roberta Stevenson, a social worker employed by the court, to study the situation and to make recommendations to him as to what he should decide. Roberta, who had special training regarding lesbian adoptions, recommended to

66

Judge Watson that Virginia should have major visitation rights because she has been a significant parental figure and that the best interest of the child is best served by a two-parent relationship. However, the judge has views not supported by the history and behaviors of all involved. The prevailing community belief is that children raised by lesbians suffer harm, and Judge Watson believes that having a lesbian parent—whatever the legalities—will by itself affect a child's sexual identity, lead to peer rejection, or expose the child to unusual images of family life. He thinks that to allow Virginia visitation rights would only make a bad situation worse and there is room in the law for leeway for his decision. How would you handle this as a social worker?

Step 1: Divide into dyads. Using the ERS (figure 4.2) and EPS (figure 4.2) in Chapter 4 answer the following questions about the above scenario:

Step 2: Consult the evidence which will either support or negate the Judge's decision

Step 3: Discuss with your classmates how you will frame the evidence you have found on this topic to persuade the Judge to see your point of view about the welfare of the child.

Exercise 5: Who is Correct?

Focus Competencies/Practice Behaviors:

EP 2.1.2 Apply social work ethical principles to guide professional practice
d. Apply strategies of ethical reasoning to arrive at principled decisions

GOAL: *This exercise is designed to help social worker's understand that there can be several answers to a dilemma that are essentially ethically sound. In these cases problem solving should be utilized to choose the most effective solution*

Early last year, more than 400 new Central American refugee families arrived in Westport. Centro Latino was able to generate a special onetime $100,000 grant to help in the adjustment of these refugees. The board of directors decided after lengthy discussion to allocate 20% of this grant to employ two more part-time social workers and to distribute the remaining funds directly to families to help them in their adjustment. The detailed rules for distributing these funds were to be developed by the agency's staff. The current staff meeting was devoted to developing criteria for distributing the funds. The agency's director, Sandra Lopez, argued that equity demanded that each of the families receive an equal cash grant of approximately $200, which each family could use as it wished. Several staff members agreed with Sandra. But others urged that the limited funds be used where they could do the most good. Since the basic needs were already met, the new monies should be earmarked for special needs where an intensive use of resources could best achieve the desired objective. Each staff group

67

believed that its proposal was professionally sound and supported by the professional ethics code.

Step 1: Divide into two groups.

Step 2: Consult the NASW Code of Ethics regarding this issue. Consult your text – figures 4.2 and 4.3 and utilize the Ethical Assessments to help guide your answer.

Step 3: After you are fully prepared engage in a debate about this issue each group taking one of the sides discussed above.

Role-Play

Exercise A: Duty to Protect

<u>Focus Competencies/Practice Behaviors:</u>

EP 2.1.2 Apply social work ethical principles to guide professional practice
a. Recognize and manage personal values in a way that allows professional values to guide practice
d. Apply strategies of ethical reasoning to arrive at principled decisions

<u>GOAL:</u> *To be aware that in addition to varying state legislation and court decisions concerning the duty to protect, a fundamental issue of concern is the assessment of the probability of violence.*

Thomas Wayland is a resident of Room 209 in the Serenity Nursing Home. His roommate
has a serious cognitive impairment, is generally incompetent, is incontinent, and makes continual repetitive noises that Thomas finds deeply disturbing. He spoke to a nurse's aide a week ago requesting that his room be changed. He repeated his request to that aide and several others, but so far there have been no changes. This morning he asked that his social worker, Kelli Forsbeck, come visit him. When Kelli arrived, Thomas was quite disturbed and angry; he explained to her that he had asked several times over a full week for a change of room, but nothing had been done to correct his situation. All of his requests have been ignored. He is still in the same room with the same roommate and the same noises. Kelli said she would speak to the head nurse to ask if his room can be changed. When she did so, she was told that the home has no beds available to meet Thomas's request. There are a number of people waiting to be admitted to the home. Other residents also have made requests that cannot be met at this time. Furthermore, she noted, the problem is not unique to Thomas and his current roommate. Other residents also have disconcerting and annoying characteristics, so there is no assurance that if Thomas is moved he will go to a room without some disturbance. She suggested impatiently that Kelli calm Thomas as best she can and when Kelli persisted in advocating with the head nurse, the nurse became visibly upset. Kelli is torn. Was the nurse's comment a threat about her job? Other residents also have needs that are unmet.

Step 1: Divide into dyads. One student will role play the social worker and the other Jillian the supervisor.

Step 2: The goal is to help the clients as well as the supervisor and the agency.

Step 3: Discuss your experiences with your classmates.

Name: _____ **Date:** _____

Supervisor's Name: _____

Focus Competencies/Practice Behaviors:

EP 2.1.2 Apply social work ethical principles to guide professional practice
a. Recognize and manage personal values in a way that allows professional values to guide practice
d. Apply strategies of ethical reasoning to arrive at principled decisions

EP 2.1.4 Engage Diversity and Difference in Practice
b. Gain sufficient self-awareness to eliminate the influence of personal biases and values in working with diverse groups

Instructions:

A. Evaluate your work or your partner's work in the Focus Competencies/Practice Behaviors by completing the Competencies/Practice Behaviors Assessment form below
B. What other Competencies/Practice Behaviors did you use to complete these Exercises? Be sure to record them in your assessments

1.	I have attained this competency/practice behavior (in the range of 81 to 100%)
2.	I have largely attained this competency/practice behavior (in the range of 61 to 80%)
3.	I have partially attained this competency/practice behavior (in the range of 41 to 60%)
4.	I have made a little progress in attaining this competency/practice behavior (in the range of 21 to 40%)
5.	I have made almost no progress in attaining this competency/practice behavior (in the range of 0 to 20%)

Student and Evaluator Assessment Scale and Comments	0	1	2	3	4	5	Agree/Disagree/Comments
EP 2.1.1 Identify as a Professional Social Worker and Conduct Oneself Accordingly							
a. Advocate for client access to the services of social work							
b. Practice personal reflection and self-correction to assure continual professional development							
c. Attend to professional roles and boundaries							
d. Demonstrate professional demeanor in behavior, appearance, and communication							
e. Engage in career-long learning							
f. Use supervision and consultation							

EP 2.1.2 Apply Social Work Ethical Principles to Guide Professional Practice							
a.	Recognize and manage personal values in a way that allows professional values to guide practice						
b.	Make ethical decisions by applying NASW Code of Ethics and, as applicable, of the IFSW/IASSW Ethics in Social Work, Statement of Principles						
c.	Tolerate ambiguity in resolving ethical conflicts						
d.	Apply strategies of ethical reasoning to arrive at principled decisions						

EP 2.1.3 Apply Critical Thinking to Inform and Communicate Professional Judgments							
a.	Distinguish, appraise, and integrate multiple sources of knowledge, including research-based knowledge and practice wisdom						
b.	Analyze models of assessment, prevention, intervention, and evaluation						
c.	Demonstrate effective oral and written communication in working with individuals, families, groups, organizations, communities, and colleagues						
EP 2.1.4 Engage Diversity and Difference in Practice							
a.	Recognize the extent to which a culture's structures and values may oppress, marginalize, alienate, or create or enhance privilege and power						
b.	Gain sufficient self-awareness to eliminate the influence of personal biases and values in working with diverse groups						
c.	Recognize and communicate their understanding of the importance of difference in shaping life experiences						
d.	View themselves as learners and engage those with whom they work as informants						
EP 2.1.5 Advance Human Rights and Social and Economic Justice							
a.	Understand forms and mechanisms of oppression and discrimination						
b.	Advocate for human rights and social and economic justice						
c.	Engage in practices that advance social and economic justice						
EP 2.1.6 Engage in Research-Informed Practice and Practice-Informed Research							
a.	Use practice experience to inform scientific inquiry						
b.	Use research evidence to inform practice						

71

EP 2.1.7 Apply Knowledge of Human Behavior and the Social Environment							
a.	Utilize conceptual frameworks to guide the processes of assessment, intervention, and evaluation						
b.	Critique and apply knowledge to understand person and environment						
EP 2.1.8 Engage in Policy Practice to Advance Social and Economic Well-Being and to Deliver Effective Social Work Services							
a.	Analyze, formulate, and advocate for policies that advance social well-being						
b.	Collaborate with colleagues and clients for effective policy action						
EP 2.1.9 Respond to Contexts that Shape Practice							
a.	Continuously discover, appraise, and attend to changing locales, populations, scientific and technological developments, and emerging societal trends to provide relevant services						
b.	Provide leadership in promoting sustainable changes in service delivery and practice to improve the quality of social services						
EP 2.1.10 Engage, Assess, Intervene, and Evaluate with Individuals, Families, Groups, Organizations and Communities							
a.	Substantively and affectively prepare for action with individuals, families, groups, organizations, and communities						
b.	Use empathy and other interpersonal skills						
c.	Develop a mutually agreed-on focus of work and desired outcomes						
d.	Collect, organize, and interpret client data						
e.	Assess client strengths and limitations						
f.	Develop mutually agreed-on intervention goals and objectives						
g.	Select appropriate intervention strategies						
h.	Initiate actions to achieve organizational goals						
i.	Implement prevention interventions that enhance client capacities						
j.	Help clients resolve problems						
k.	Negotiate, mediate, and advocate for clients						
l.	Facilitate transitions and endings						
m.	Critically analyze, monitor, and evaluate interventions						

Chapter 10

Organizational and Work Relationships

Exercise 1: Which Opinion Should be Utilized?

Focus Competencies/Practice Behaviors:

EP 2.1.3 Apply Critical Thinking to Inform and Communicate Professional Judgments
a. Distinguish, appraise, and integrate multiple sources of knowledge, including research based knowledge, and practice wisdom
b. Analyze models of assessment, prevention, intervention, and evaluations

GOAL: *For social workers to understand that it is incumbent on them to utilize critical thinking skills to include evidence based research to analyze assessment, prevention, intervention, and evaluation models.*

> David lives a in a residential institution. He has been diagnosed with severe attention deficit hyperactivity disorder (ADHD) and in the last few weeks, his acting out behavior has become especially problematic. He frequently tosses food during meals at other children, short sheets other children's beds, turns on fire alarms, arrives late wherever he is expected, throws pencils in class, and other such behaviors. Although he is not physically harmful to himself or others, he has been highly disruptive of the institution's daily routine. The consulting physician has prescribed medication to calm David and make him easier to manage, but the cottage social worker has refused on ethical grounds to administer this medicine to David. She feels strongly that such pharmaceutical control will interfere with the child's welfare and freedom and will be counterproductive in any therapy attempted. Her social work supervisor supports this decision. The physician insists the medication prescribed be given to David. The institution's director, a psychologist supports the doctor against the decision of the social worker.

Step 1: Review the NASW Code of Ethics with regard to this issue.

Step 2: Using the problem solving processes from your text, decide on the course of action you would take in this social worker's position.

Exercise 2: Questionable Conduct

Focus Competencies/Practice Behaviors:

EP 2.1.2 Apply social work ethical principles to guide professional practice
d. Apply strategies of ethical reasoning to arrive at principled decisions

<u>GOAL</u>: *To assist students in conducting an exhaustive query should a colleague's conduct come into question.*

Your colleague Mitchell Moore has been hospitalized quite suddenly. While he is on sick leave, you have been assigned to cover some of his cases. You learn from one of his clients that Mitch has threatened to report one of his clients to Child Protective Services if she does not help him obtain illegal drugs. She says that she was uncomfortable complying with his request but was afraid she would lose her children if she didn't do as Mitch asked. She also asks you to protect her confidentiality and that she will handle the situation when he returns. This behavior is clearly illegal and in violation of the Code.

Step 1: Review page 197 of your text. What should be your goal as the social worker who is receiving this information?

Step 2: Decide on your objective(s).

Step 3: Decide if your client's report is trustworthy, and ask yourself if you can you/or should act if you have questions about what happened.

Step 4: If you believe the client's reports consider the issues one by one, but not in any order of priority.

Step 5: Write a report about how you would handle this situation.

Exercise 3: Failure to Report a Case of Child Abuse

<u>Focus Competencies/Practice Behaviors:</u>

EP 2.1.2 Apply social work ethical principles to guide professional practice
d. Apply strategies of ethical reasoning to arrive at principled decisions

<u>GOAL</u>: *To help students understand the necessity of reporting suspected child abuse.*

Jake Dember, a frail 5 year old, was brought to the emergency room of Mt. Ebal Hospital unconscious, covered with blood from head to toe, with severe internal injuries. His father, Hiram, said that Jake fell from their second-floor apartment and   landed headfirst on the cement sidewalk. The medical team was able to save Jake's life, though serious brain damage could not be reversed. Now, two weeks later, Jake is still in the hospital's critical care unit. The attending physicians are going to report this as a case of child abuse. Before doing so, they have asked the hospital social worker, Josie Perry, to pull together all the relevant information they possess so that it can be provided to child protective services (CPS) at the time of the report. Erica Dember, Jake's mother, did not want to talk to Josie. She said that she and her husband were already in family therapy at the family service agency, and if Josie wanted to know anything about them, she should talk to their therapist, Ed Custer. Josie arranged to meet with Ed on the following afternoon. He was willing to share his assessment of the Dember family because both parents had signed the customary consent forms when Jake was admitted to the hospital. In the course of their conversation, Ed acknowledged that he had been aware of ongoing child abuse in this family, but because he thought that it was not too serious, he did not file a report. He feared that such a report would have interfered with the therapeutic relationship that he was trying to develop with this family.

Step 1: Answer the following questions:

1. How should Josie Perry resolve the ethical dilemma facing her?
2. Should she report Ed's negligence to the NASW chapter? Ignore it? Choose another action?

Step 2: Return to page 197 of your text and use the problem solving approach of deciding the goal, objective(s), and method or decision making.

| Exercise 4: Who is Being Served? |

Focus Competencies/Practice Behaviors:

EP 2.1.2 Apply social work ethical principles to guide professional practice
d. Apply strategies of ethical reasoning to arrive at principled decisions

GOAL: *This exercise is designed to help social workers analyze how agency and state policies affect budgets and ultimately the clients that they serve.*

> Terry Newton is a social worker in a private organization, Upward Strivers that performs contract work for a local Department of Social Services (DSS). The clients receive public assistance under the Temporary Assistance to Needy Families (TANF) program as long as they are enrolled and active in a program that is designed to prepare them for regular employment through job readiness training. When needed, clients also receive GED preparation or literacy classes. After completing the three weeks of job readiness, those clients not enrolled in training programs must begin job searches with the help of a placement specialist and may be enrolled part time in GED preparation or literacy training. The Department of Social Services frequently refers pregnant women to the job readiness program. None of these women are able to find employment following the training because most employers won't hire pregnant women. The pregnant women are enrolled in GED preparation in order to avoid the loss of their financial support. Both Upward Strivers and the DSS created this informal policy, which enables both DSS and Upward Strivers to receive payments from the state even though this informal policy is not consistent with the official state policy.

75

The purpose of these informal policies is to maintain payments for the client, the Upward Strivers, and the DSS. The client needs financial support as do the two agencies, both of which are engaged in many important and constructive activities. Whose purpose is being served here? What should you do as a social worker observing these policies (if anything)?

Step 1: Divide into dyads. Using the ERS (figure 4.2) and EPS (figure 4.2) in Chapter 4 answer the following questions about the above scenario:

Step 2: For a grade, write your answers and show how you used the Assessments to come to your conclusions.

Step 3: Discuss your answers with the rest of the class.

Exercise 5: Outreach for Archie

Focus Competencies/Practice Behaviors:

EP 2.1.2 Apply social work ethical principles to guide professional practice
d. Apply strategies of ethical reasoning to arrive at principled decisions

GOAL: *This exercise is designed to help social workers consider how circumstance in various organizations including the military impacts a social worker's priorities.*

Sergeant Richard Mozart recently discussed some personal difficulties with Captain Emilio Pacifico, a social worker on an army base. Sgt. Mozart is assigned to hazardous duty and told Capt. Pacifico that he is a moderate alcohol user. Capt. Pacifico was recently transferred to a new duty station. As a result, he transferred Sgt. Mozart's case file to the new social worker assigned to the base. When the newly assigned social worker—Lt. Ted Maddox—read the file, he reported Sgt. Mozart and had him taken off hazardous duty; he did not consult with Capt. Pacifico or talk to Sgt. Mozart before making this report. As a result of this, Sgt. Mozart filed an ethics complaint against Capt. Pacifico.

Step 1: Consider the following: Balancing the needs of the individual and the needs of the unit and its mission is an important challenge. For military social workers, achieving the unit's mission has become the priority value, so that the traditional social work values such as self-determination and clinical judgment become a lower-rank imperative.

Step 2: Using figures 4.2 and 4.3 begin the process of problem solving how you would handle this situation.

Step 3: Divide into dyads and discuss this scenario and the process your group would take in this situation.

Role-Play

Exercise A: Serving Only the Good People

Focus Competencies/Practice Behaviors:

EP 2.1.2 Apply social work ethical principles to guide professional practice
a. Recognize and manage personal values in a way that allows professional values to guide practice
d. Apply strategies of ethical reasoning to arrive at principled decisions

GOAL: *To learn to use the problem solving process to arrive at principled decisions.*

Amanda Frankel is a social worker for an international aid organization in a war zone. The forces of one side of the conflict are particularly cruel, attacking civilians, raping young girls and older women, and murdering groups of men and burying their bodies to do away with evidence. Until yesterday, Amanda was happy and proud to serve those in need who were being attacked. Then her supervisor sent a message that she was going to be transferred to the other side to serve the people there. Just as here, she would serve all people, including military and paramilitary personnel. She was awake all night considering what she should do.

Step 1: Divide into dyads. One student should role play Amanda and another Amanda's social work colleague.

Step 2: When role playing these social workers answer the following: What is the ethically correct choice in this situation? In what way is Ethical Principle 2 (social justice) relevant to Amanda's situation and dilemma? In what ways do her personal values conflict with her employing agency's values and requirements? Does the NASW (2008) Code of Ethics suggest there is a correct choice for Amanda? Can you identify in your local community situations in which social workers might have their personal values challenged by similar decisions by the
agencies for which they work?

Chapter 10
Competencies/Practice Behaviors Exercises Assessment:

Name: _____   **Date:** _____

Supervisor's Name: _____

Focus Competencies/Practice Behaviors:

EP 2.1.2 Apply social work ethical principles to guide professional practice
a. Recognize and manage personal values in a way that allows professional values to guide practice
d. Apply strategies of ethical reasoning to arrive at principled decisions

EP 2.1.3 Apply Critical Thinking to Inform and Communicate Professional Judgments
a. Distinguish, appraise, and integrate multiple sources of knowledge, including research based knowledge, and practice wisdom
b. Analyze models of assessment, prevention, intervention, and evaluations

Instructions:

A.   Evaluate your work or your partner's work in the Focus Competencies/Practice Behaviors by completing the Competencies/Practice Behaviors Assessment form below

B.   What other Competencies/Practice Behaviors did you use to complete these Exercises? Be sure to record them in your assessments

1.	I have attained this competency/practice behavior (in the range of 81 to 100%)
2.	I have largely attained this competency/practice behavior (in the range of 61 to 80%)
3.	I have partially attained this competency/practice behavior (in the range of 41 to 60%)
4.	I have made a little progress in attaining this competency/practice behavior (in the range of 21 to 40%)
5.	I have made almost no progress in attaining this competency/practice behavior (in the range of 0 to 20%)

Student and Evaluator Assessment Scale and Comments	0	1	2	3	4	5	Agree/Disagree/Comments
EP 2.1.1 Identify as a Professional Social Worker and Conduct Oneself Accordingly							
a. Advocate for client access to the services of social work							
b. Practice personal reflection and self-correction to assure continual professional development							
c. Attend to professional roles and boundaries							
d. Demonstrate professional demeanor in behavior, appearance, and communication							
e. Engage in career-long learning							
f. Use supervision and consultation							

EP 2.1.2 Apply Social Work Ethical Principles to Guide Professional Practice							
a.	Recognize and manage personal values in a way that allows professional values to guide practice						
b.	Make ethical decisions by applying NASW Code of Ethics and, as applicable, of the IFSW/IASSW Ethics in Social Work, Statement of Principles						
c.	Tolerate ambiguity in resolving ethical conflicts						
d.	Apply strategies of ethical reasoning to arrive at principled decisions						

EP 2.1.3 Apply Critical Thinking to Inform and Communicate Professional Judgments							
a.	Distinguish, appraise, and integrate multiple sources of knowledge, including research-based knowledge and practice wisdom						
b.	Analyze models of assessment, prevention, intervention, and evaluation						
c.	Demonstrate effective oral and written communication in working with individuals, families, groups, organizations, communities, and colleagues						
EP 2.1.4 Engage Diversity and Difference in Practice							
a.	Recognize the extent to which a culture's structures and values may oppress, marginalize, alienate, or create or enhance privilege and power						
b.	Gain sufficient self-awareness to eliminate the influence of personal biases and values in working with diverse groups						
c.	Recognize and communicate their understanding of the importance of difference in shaping life experiences						
d.	View themselves as learners and engage those with whom they work as informants						
EP 2.1.5 Advance Human Rights and Social and Economic Justice							
a.	Understand forms and mechanisms of oppression and discrimination						
b.	Advocate for human rights and social and economic justice						
c.	Engage in practices that advance social and economic justice						
EP 2.1.6 Engage in Research-Informed Practice and Practice-Informed Research							
a.	Use practice experience to inform scientific inquiry						
b.	Use research evidence to inform practice						

EP 2.1.7 Apply Knowledge of Human Behavior and the Social Environment						
a. Utilize conceptual frameworks to guide the processes of assessment, intervention, and evaluation						
b. Critique and apply knowledge to understand person and environment						
EP 2.1.8 Engage in Policy Practice to Advance Social and Economic Well-Being and to Deliver Effective Social Work Services						
a. Analyze, formulate, and advocate for policies that advance social well-being						
b. Collaborate with colleagues and clients for effective policy action						
EP 2.1.9 Respond to Contexts that Shape Practice						
a. Continuously discover, appraise, and attend to changing locales, populations, scientific and technological developments, and emerging societal trends to provide relevant services						
b. Provide leadership in promoting sustainable changes in service delivery and practice to improve the quality of social services						
EP 2.1.10 Engage, Assess, Intervene, and Evaluate with Individuals, Families, Groups, Organizations and Communities						
a. Substantively and affectively prepare for action with individuals, families, groups, organizations, and communities						
b. Use empathy and other interpersonal skills						
c. Develop a mutually agreed-on focus of work and desired outcomes						
d. Collect, organize, and interpret client data						
e. Assess client strengths and limitations						
f. Develop mutually agreed-on intervention goals and objectives						
g. Select appropriate intervention strategies						
h. Initiate actions to achieve organizational goals						
i. Implement prevention interventions that enhance client capacities						
j. Help clients resolve problems						
k. Negotiate, mediate, and advocate for clients						
l. Facilitate transitions and endings						
m. Critically analyze, monitor, and evaluate interventions						

Chapter 11

Social Work with Selected Client Groups

Exercise 1: Cultural Understanding

Focus Competencies/Practice Behaviors:

EP 2.1.1 Identify as a Professional Social Worker and Conduct Oneself Accordingly
a. Advocate for client access to the services of social work
c. Attend to professional roles and boundaries
d. Demonstrate professional demeanor in behavior, appearance, and communication

GOAL: This exercise is designed to help students understand that *sensitive and informed social work practice can demand that social workers practice in various and counterintuitive ways, ways that may be considered unethical..*

> Hyun Cho, an Asian American and recent immigrant in her early 50s, was referred to the Western Neighborhood Counseling Center by a non-Asian friend whom she admired and who had been helped at the Center. Hyun explained to Haley Traylor, her social worker, that she started having stomachaches, accompanied by becoming quite anxious, following her husband's being laid off. A visit to a physician found no physical problems. As treatment proceeded, things went quite well for a time, and Hyun began to feel better and more in control of her life. At that point Hyun told Haley that although she is feeling better, a woman at her church told her she should not be using the Western Neighborhood Counseling Center but should use Asian methods and Asian persons to deal with her problems. Hyun announced that she appreciates the help she has been given, but she thinks her friend is correct and intends to go to a healer who emphasizes meditation and green tea. This decision surprised Haley because she had heard that the particular healer Hyun is going to visit is not helpful and that several persons had their physical problems worsen after his treatment.

Step 1: Using figures 4.2 and 4.3 from your text answer the following questions:

1. What is the ethical choice for Haley?
2. Should she tell Hyun what she knows about other persons' experiences with the neighborhood healer?
3. Would that lead to an informed choice?
4. Should she remain silent about her knowledge and accept without question Hyun's decision?

Step 2: Divide into two groups. Each group should write down their responses and the approach they used to reach their decisions.

Exercise 2: Conflicting Values

Focus Competencies/Practice Behaviors:

EP 2.1.2 Apply Social Work Ethical Principles to Guide Professional Practice
d. Apply strategies of ethical reasoning to arrive at principled decisions

GOAL: *This exercise is designed to reflect the rapidly expanding use of e-mail and because it raises some issues that social workers must consider.*

> A university student used an electronic mail discussion group to inquire about a drug that could be used for a painless suicide. A professor in Europe who read this request communicated his concern to the sender's university, which forwarded this message to the university's counseling department. The counselor assigned to this case obtained more information before deciding what to do. She contacted the director of the computer center, who broke into the student's account where additional messages on suicide were discovered. At this point, the counselor decided to contact the student's parents. (This situation was described on a social work electronic discussion list and is used with permission of Steve Marson of Pembroke University. The counselor was not a social worker.)

Step 1: Ask the students to read the chapter in the NASW Code of Ethics that discusses issues of confidentiality.

Step 2: Ask the students to consider questions regarding the circumstances under which a social worker should seek access to a confidential electronic file. Is there any issue short of life-threatening situations that might support such an action? Under what circumstances does the computer center or a social agency have a right to examine someone's personal computer account?

Step 3: After sufficient time to review the NASW Code of Ethics have a group discussion the actions of the counselor.

Exercise 3: Critical Thinking

Focus Competencies/Practice Behaviors:

EP 2.1.3 Apply Critical Thinking to Inform and Communicate Professional Judgments
a. Distinguish, appraise, and integrate multiple sources of knowledge, including research based knowledge, and practice wisdom
b. Analyze models of assessment, prevention, intervention, and evaluations

GOAL: *This exercise highlights ethical dilemmas that can arise when conflicting groups assert privileges over the social worker's allegiance.*

Evelyn Waters was on a home visit with Mr. Lee when he asked her to contact a shaman (a member of certain tribal societies who acts as a medium between the visible and spirit worlds for healing, divination, or control over events) because he has been feeling quite ill. When the social worker instead suggested he should be taken to a local walk-in clinic, he was very resistant and insisted on seeing a shaman. Because the client was conscious and seemed to be in control, Ms. Waters decided to take the phone number and called the shaman, who said he would come immediately. When the shaman arrived, he spoke to Mr. Lee briefly in private and then started the healing process by looping a coiled thread around Mr. Lee's wrist. The shaman explained that he was summoning Mr. Lee's runaway soul. In addition, the shaman traced with his finger a protective invisible shield around Mr. Lee. Given Mr. Lee's history of diabetes and hypertension, Ms. Waters was concerned that the shaman's treatment might not be sufficient or may even be harmful.

Step 1: Using the problem solving process described in figures 4.2 and 4.3 answer the following questions in a two page paper:

1. Is it helpful to know that Hmong people rely on their spiritual beliefs to get them through illnesses?
2. Was it ethical to accept Mr. Lee's self-determination and assessment of his situation?
3. What ethical alternatives existed before calling the shaman, after his arrival, and after his treatment began?
4. Would it make a difference if the shaman decided to treat Mr. Lee in his own way and insisted Mr. Lee could be brought to the clinic but not before tomorrow morning?

Exercise 4: Diversity and Difference in Social Work Practice

Focus Competencies/Practice Behaviors:

EP 2.1.4 Engage diversity and difference in practice
b. Gain sufficient self-awareness to eliminate the influence of personal biases and values in working with diverse groups

GOAL: *This exercise is designed to help students gain sufficient awareness to eliminate the influence of personal biases and values when working with diverse clients.*

You are providing supervision to a BSW student in a mental health agency. Your student was assigned a 17 year old client who is pregnant and seeking an abortion. The social work student is tasked with case management in helping the client find a reputable clinic in addition to mental health after care. Your student has asked to be relieved of the assignment and is asking for a different placement because she believes the agency is evil in its support of abortions.

Step 1: Refer to pages 232-233 in your text and read RELIGION, SOCIAL WORK VALUES, AND SECULARISM.

Step 2: Divide into groups of 3 or 4 and discuss how you might handle such a situation without feeling discriminatory toward the student's religious values.

Step 3: What is social work education's ethical responsibility to recognize and deal constructively with what Hodge identifies as secular privilege?

Step 4: Discuss your answers as a group.

Exercise 5: Varying Roles in Social Work Practice

Focus Competencies/Practice Behaviors:

EP 2.1.2 Apply social work ethical principles to guide professional practice
b. Make ethical decisions by applying standards of the National Association of Social Workers Code of Ethics and, as applicable, of the International Federation of Social Workers/International Association of Schools of Social Work Ethics in Social Work, Statement of Principles.

GOAL: *This exercise is designed to help students begin to understand various ethical circumstances that might occur depending on the social work role.*

Jane Addams is a social work student who is currently working in a child protective services agency for her field placement. She is so amazed about the issues that she sees during her work that she has decided to start a blog on the internet to describe various issues that she believes need to be brought to the public's attention.

Step 1: Consult the NASW Code of Ethics regarding this issue.

Step 2: As a group discusses all of the ethical concerns about Jane's decision to blog about her work.

Role-Play

Exercise A: Right to Die

Focus Competencies/Practice Behaviors:

EP 2.1.2 Apply social work ethical principles to guide professional practice
a. Recognize and manage personal values in a way that allows professional values to guide practice
d. Apply strategies of ethical reasoning to arrive at principled decisions

GOAL: To demonstrate the application of social work ethical principles that guide professional practice.

Step 1: You are a hospice social worker working with a 60 year old woman who is in the late stages of breast cancer. Her husband died approximately four years ago and although she seemed to adjust to his death she has told you that he was the "love of my life" and is requesting that you assist her in suicide. She explained that since she is suffering and would like to be with her husband you would be providing the best and most ethical treatment for her condition.

Step 2: Role play the two characters and describe your personal values as a social worker to the client. The client should be adamant about her decision and reasoning during the role play.

Name: _____ **Date:** _____

Supervisor's Name: _____

Focus Competencies/Practice Behaviors:

EP 2.1.1 Identify as a Professional Social Worker and Conduct Oneself Accordingly
a. Advocate for client access to the services of social work
c. Attend to professional roles and boundaries
d. Demonstrate professional demeanor in behavior, appearance, and communication

EP 2.1.2 Apply Social Work Ethical Principles to Guide Professional Practice
a. Recognize and manage personal values in a way that allows professional values to guide practice
b. Make ethical decisions by applying standards of the National Association of Social Workers Code of Ethics and, as applicable, of the International Federation of Social Workers/International Association of Schools of Social Work Ethics in Social Work, Statement of Principles.
d. Apply strategies of ethical reasoning to arrive at principled decisions

EP 2.1.3 Apply Critical Thinking to Inform and Communicate Professional Judgments
a. Distinguish, appraise, and integrate multiple sources of knowledge, including research based knowledge, and practice wisdom
b. Analyze models of assessment, prevention, intervention, and evaluations

EP 2.1.4 Engage Diversity and Difference in Practice
b. Gain sufficient self-awareness to eliminate the influence of personal biases and values in working with diverse groups

Instructions:

A. Evaluate your work or your partner's work in the Focus Competencies/Practice Behaviors by completing the Competencies/Practice Behaviors Assessment form below
B. What other Competencies/Practice Behaviors did you use to complete these Exercises? Be sure to record them in your assessments

1.	I have attained this competency/practice behavior (in the range of 81 to 100%)
2.	I have largely attained this competency/practice behavior (in the range of 61 to 80%)
3.	I have partially attained this competency/practice behavior (in the range of 41 to 60%)
4.	I have made a little progress in attaining this competency/practice behavior (in the range of 21 to 40%)
5.	I have made almost no progress in attaining this competency/practice behavior (in the range of 0 to 20%)

Student and Evaluator Assessment Scale and Comments	0	1	2	3	4	5	Agree/Disagree/Comments
EP 2.1.1 Identify as a Professional Social Worker and Conduct Oneself Accordingly							
a. Advocate for client access to the services of social work							
b. Practice personal reflection and self-correction to assure continual professional development							
c. Attend to professional roles and boundaries							
d. Demonstrate professional demeanor in behavior, appearance, and communication							
e. Engage in career-long learning							
f. Use supervision and consultation							
EP 2.1.2 Apply Social Work Ethical Principles to Guide Professional Practice							
a. Recognize and manage personal values in a way that allows professional values to guide practice							
b. Make ethical decisions by applying NASW Code of Ethics and, as applicable, of the IFSW/IASSW Ethics in Social Work, Statement of Principles							
c. Tolerate ambiguity in resolving ethical conflicts							
d. Apply strategies of ethical reasoning to arrive at principled decisions							

Student and Evaluator Assessment Scale and Comments	0	1	2	3	4	5	Agree/Disagree/Comments
EP 2.1.3 Apply Critical Thinking to Inform and Communicate Professional Judgments							
a. Distinguish, appraise, and integrate multiple sources of knowledge, including research-based knowledge and practice wisdom							
b. Analyze models of assessment, prevention, intervention, and evaluation							
c. Demonstrate effective oral and written communication in working with individuals, families, groups, organizations, communities, and colleagues							
EP 2.1.4 Engage Diversity and Difference in Practice							
a. Recognize the extent to which a culture's structures and values may oppress, marginalize, alienate, or create or enhance privilege and power							
b. Gain sufficient self-awareness to eliminate the influence of personal biases and values in working with diverse groups							
c. Recognize and communicate their understanding of the importance of difference in shaping life experiences							
d. View themselves as learners and engage those with whom they work as informants							

EP 2.1.5 Advance Human Rights and Social and Economic Justice							
a. Understand forms and mechanisms of oppression and discrimination							
b. Advocate for human rights and social and economic justice							
c. Engage in practices that advance social and economic justice							
EP 2.1.6 Engage in Research-Informed Practice and Practice-Informed Research							
a. Use practice experience to inform scientific inquiry							
b. Use research evidence to inform practice							
EP 2.1.7 Apply Knowledge of Human Behavior and the Social Environment							
a. Utilize conceptual frameworks to guide the processes of assessment, intervention, and evaluation							
b. Critique and apply knowledge to understand person and environment							
EP 2.1.8 Engage in Policy Practice to Advance Social and Economic Well-Being and to Deliver Effective Social Work Services							
a. Analyze, formulate, and advocate for policies that advance social well-being							
b. Collaborate with colleagues and clients for effective policy action							
EP 2.1.9 Respond to Contexts that Shape Practice							
a. Continuously discover, appraise, and attend to changing locales, populations, scientific and technological developments, and emerging societal trends to provide relevant services							
b. Provide leadership in promoting sustainable changes in service delivery and practice to improve the quality of social services							
EP 2.1.10 Engage, Assess, Intervene, and Evaluate with Individuals, Families, Groups, Organizations and Communities							
a. Substantively and affectively prepare for action with individuals, families, groups, organizations, and communities							
b. Use empathy and other interpersonal skills							
c. Develop a mutually agreed-on focus of work and desired outcomes							
d. Collect, organize, and interpret client data							
e. Assess client strengths and limitations							
f. Develop mutually agreed-on intervention goals and objectives							
g. Select appropriate intervention strategies							
h. Initiate actions to achieve organizational goals							
i. Implement prevention interventions that enhance client capacities							
j. Help clients resolve problems							
k. Negotiate, mediate, and advocate for clients							
l. Facilitate transitions and endings							
m. Critically analyze, monitor, and evaluate interventions							

Chapter 12

Changing World, Changing Dilemmas

Exercise 1: Insurance Issues

Focus Competencies or Practice Behaviors:

EP 2.1.2 Apply social work ethical principles to guide professional practice
d. Apply strategies of ethical reasoning to arrive at principled decisions

GOAL: *For social workers to understand that it is incumbent on them to take measures to protect their clients.*

> Dr. Felicia Montevideo, director of social work clinical services for Family and Children's Services of Pleasant City, was surprised when she received a letter from the Pine Tree Insurance Company (Managed Care Division) and later a phone call, both of which subtly suggested that more of the agency's treatment services be offered in time-limited groups. When she raised the issue with the agency's administrative executive committee, some argued in favor of complying because the money received from the insurance company made up a substantial part of the agency's income. Others were concerned that such a change in operating procedures would upset the staff. Still others wanted to know what would be most helpful to clients, and some argued that compliance would mean yielding their professional judgment to the Pine Tree Insurance Company. Among the options suggested by committee members are the following: (a) ignore the suggestion because it had not been explicitly stated; (b) comply as soon as possible with the suggestion; (c) refuse to comply and begin to advocate with Pine Tree Insurance for the current mix of service modalities; (d) examine and review research on the relative effectiveness of various treatment methods; and (e) meet with Pine Tree representatives to explore ways to slowly phase in more group treatment. What are the ethical implications of each option?

Step 1: How would you handle this situation?

Step 2: Divide into three groups. Each group will have a large piece of poster paper to write on. You will have 10 minutes to come up with an answer that is equitable to all parties using figures 4.2 and/or 4.3 to process this problem.

Step 3: Discuss your answers with one another.

Exercise 2: Advocacy in Social Work Practice

Focus Competencies or Practice Behaviors:

2.1.5 Advance Human Rights and Social and Economic Justice
a. Understand forms and mechanisms of oppression and discrimination
b. Advocate for human rights and social and economic justice
c. Engage in practices that advance social and economic justice

GOAL: *To understand problem solving on a macro level to enhance client advocacy.*

Anita Dee is a social worker in a state psychiatric hospital that primarily serves low income people of color. The Medicaid recipients are served through a managed care system that is privately operated. Generally, administrators and supervisors in this public hospital seek harmonious relationships with the managed care organization, located in another state. Anita recently realized that when chronically ill psychiatric patients are discharged, the managed care company refers them to outpatient sites that are seldom near where they reside and transportation to the treatment sites is not provided. Consequently, the discharged persons are not receiving the help they need. Anita believes the managed care company is discriminating against poor and minority person because there are services available closer to clients' homes, but these services are not allowed because they are more expensive. Anita would like to challenge the managed care organization's decisions, but her supervisor says her job is to help prepare persons to leave the hospital and anything after that is not her concern.

Step 1: Consult the NASW Code of Ethics regarding discriminatory practices and consult your text regarding this scenario.

Step 2: Write a one page paper about the process you would use to remedy this issue.

Exercise 3: Can Deception be Justified?

Focus Competencies or Practice Behaviors:

EP 2.1.2 Apply social work ethical principles to guide professional practice
d. Apply strategies of ethical reasoning to arrive at principled decisions

GOAL: *To exam situations where an ethical social worker wants to serve clients who can no longer pay for services.*

Larry Firth came to consult with you about a difficult family situation. His wife has left him and their two sons in order to live with her boyfriend. He himself has formed a relationship with a married neighbor. However, he is concerned what his teenage sons will say and do when they find out the truth about their parents. You are making good progress in helping Larry come to grips with his problem. Today, however, Larry tells you that he has lost his job and can no longer afford to pay for counseling. What should you do?

Step 1: Consult the NASW Code of Ethics regarding conflict with agency policies or relevant laws or regulations.

Step2: Define the ethical issue(s)

Step 3: Give all possible solutions to the issue(s) at hand using the NASW Code of Ethics as a guide.

Exercise 4: Addressing Discriminatory Practice

Focus Competencies or Practice Behaviors:

EP 2.1.2 Apply social work ethical principles to guide professional practice
d. Apply strategies of ethical reasoning to arrive at principled decisions

GOAL: *This exercise is designed to help social workers understand the need to use evidence in all areas of practice.*

One of Sheryl Hall's clients, Claire Johnson, was referred to her after Claire's physician made a diagnosis of depression. Claire's physician wanted to prescribe an antidepressant, but Claire refused to take the medication prescribed. She is afraid that the medicine will harm her 3-month-old baby because she is breastfeeding, and she previously had been prescribed medications for depression that made her life miserable with headaches, dry mouth, and sweating. Because of Claire's refusal to take the antidepressants, her physician referred her to Sheryl for counseling. He expected Sheryl to convince Claire to take her medication. The physician expressed great concern about the infant's health. Sheryl has little experience treating depression, but there are no other licensed social workers in the area. At the first session, Claire stated that she is very concerned that, due to her depression, she is not adequately caring for her baby and that she needs immediate relief so she can be a better mother, but she cannot cope with the side effects of the medication. How would you handle this as a social worker?

Step 1: Divide into dyads. Using the ERS (figure 4.2) and EPS (figure 4.2) find the most amicable solution to this ethical dilemma.

Step 3: Discuss with your classmates how you will handle this situation.

Exercise 5: Who is Correct?

Focus Competencies or Practice Behaviors:

EP 2.1.2 Apply Social Work Ethical Principles to Guide Professional Practice
a. Recognize and manage personal values in a way that allows professional values to guide practice
b. Make ethical decisions by applying standards of the National Association of Social Workers Code of Ethics and, as applicable, of the International Federation of Social Workers/International Association of Schools of Social Work Ethics in Social Work, Statement of Principles
c. Tolerate ambiguity in resolving ethical conflicts
d. Apply strategies of ethical reasoning to arrive at principled decisions

GOAL: *This exercise is designed to help social worker's understand that there can be several answers to a dilemma that are essentially ethically sound. In these cases problem solving should be utilized to choose the most effective solution*

> Valerie Crowe, the lone social worker and counselor at Littleton Community College, teaches Human Behavior 101 and works in the Student Counseling Center. Littleton Community College is in a remote mountainous section of a western state approximately 75 miles from Bigton, the nearest town with mental health services other than those offered at the community college. Today, when Valerie went to the counseling center, she found that she was scheduled to meet with Raymond Silver, a student in her Human Behavior 101 class. He told her that he has been having very disturbing thoughts about his inadequacies and feelings of guilt that are making it difficult for him to study and to sleep. Valerie made a judgment that additional assessment and possible treatment was needed. Valerie was conflicted about whether it would be appropriate for her to provide assessment and counseling services to one of her students, but she is the only counselor at the center and based on her prior experiences, getting an appointment to see a psychiatrist in Bigton would take at least two months. Even then, seeing the psychiatrist would require Raymond driving through snow on icy roads to reach the appointment.

Step 1: Divide into two groups.

Step 2: Consult the NASW Code of Ethics regarding this issue. Consult your text – figures 4.2 and 4.3 and utilize the Ethical Assessments to help guide your answer.

Step 3: Discuss your solutions as a class.

92

Role-Play

Exercise A: Best Services for a Community

Focus Competencies or Practice Behaviors:

EP 2.1.2 Apply social work ethical principles to guide professional practice
a. Recognize and manage personal values in a way that allows professional values to guide practice
d. Apply strategies of ethical reasoning to arrive at principled decisions

GOAL: *To be aware that in addition to varying state legislation and court decisions concerning the duty to protect, a fundamental issue of concern is the assessment of the probability of violence.*

You are the director of social work in a large urban community hospital located in a low-income area serving people from various economic levels. You have been assigned to staff the planning committee charged with creating a plan for the future of the hospital. You grew up in the community and have family and long-standing friends who reside there. You also have relationships with many community human service administrators and staff members. As the planning process proceeds, it becomes clear that most committee members favor the creation of a specialized cancer treatment unit, which will gain status and recognition for the hospital and also attract patients from throughout the state. Such a recommendation, however, will make it impossible to recommend improvements for emergency and ambulatory care that are desperately needed by the neighborhood. A recommendation for a cancer treatment unit will change the nature of the available health care, who will get the jobs, use of community space, kinds of housing that will be available, and so forth. It becomes clear to you that the local community will gain very little and may lose much if a cancer treatment unit is installed. You are torn between loyalties to the hospital, to the community in general, to the social and human service agencies in the community, and to the community's population, including your friends and relatives who need a different type of service.

Step 1: Divide into dyads. One student will role play the director of social work and the other student will play the administrator of the community human services administration who wants the treatment center established.

Step 2: Discuss what happened during your role play and describe your solution.

Chapter 12

Competencies/Practice Behaviors Exercises Assessment:

Name: _____ Date: _____

Supervisor's Name: _____

Focus Competencies/Practice Behaviors:

EP 2.1.2 Apply Social Work Ethical Principles to Guide Professional Practice
a. Tolerate ambiguity in resolving ethical conflicts
b. Apply strategies of ethical reasoning to arrive at principled decisions
c. Distinguish, appraise, and integrate multiple sources of knowledge, including research based knowledge, and practice wisdom.
d. Make ethical decisions by applying standards of the National Association of Social Workers Code of Ethics and, as applicable, of the International Federation of Social Workers/International Association of Schools of Social Work Ethics in Social Work, Statement of Principles
e. Analyze models of assessment, prevention, intervention, and evaluation

EP 2.1.5 Advance Human Rights and Social and Economic Justice
a. Understand forms and mechanisms of oppression and discrimination
b. Advocate for human rights and social and economic justice
c. Engage in practices that advance social and economic justice

Instructions:

A.   Evaluate your work or your partner's work in the Focus Competencies/Practice Behaviors by completing the Competencies/Practice Behaviors Assessment form below
B.   What other Competencies/Practice Behaviors did you use to complete these Exercises? Be sure to record them in your assessments

1.	I have attained this competency/practice behavior (in the range of 81 to 100%)
2.	I have largely attained this competency/practice behavior (in the range of 61 to 80%)
3.	I have partially attained this competency/practice behavior (in the range of 41 to 60%)
4.	I have made a little progress in attaining this competency/practice behavior (in the range of 21 to 40%)
5.	I have made almost no progress in attaining this competency/practice behavior (in the range of 0 to 20%)

		0	1	2	3	4	5	Agree/Disagree/Comments
EP 2.1.1 Identify as a Professional Social Worker and Conduct Oneself Accordingly								
a.	Advocate for client access to the services of social work							
b.	Practice personal reflection and self-correction to assure continual professional development							
c.	Attend to professional roles and boundaries							
d.	Demonstrate professional demeanor in behavior, appearance, and communication							

94

e.	Engage in career-long learning						
f.	Use supervision and consultation						
EP 2.1.2 Apply Social Work Ethical Principles to Guide Professional Practice							
a.	Recognize and manage personal values in a way that allows professional values to guide practice						
b.	Make ethical decisions by applying NASW Code of Ethics and, as applicable, of the IFSW/IASSW Ethics in Social Work, Statement of Principles						
c.	Tolerate ambiguity in resolving ethical conflicts						
d.	Apply strategies of ethical reasoning to arrive at principled decisions						

EP 2.1.3 Apply Critical Thinking to Inform and Communicate Professional Judgments							
a.	Distinguish, appraise, and integrate multiple sources of knowledge, including research-based knowledge and practice wisdom						
b.	Analyze models of assessment, prevention, intervention, and evaluation						
c.	Demonstrate effective oral and written communication in working with individuals, families, groups, organizations, communities, and colleagues						
EP 2.1.4 Engage Diversity and Difference in Practice							
a.	Recognize the extent to which a culture's structures and values may oppress, marginalize, alienate, or create or enhance privilege and power						
b.	Gain sufficient self-awareness to eliminate the influence of personal biases and values in working with diverse groups						
c.	Recognize and communicate their understanding of the importance of difference in shaping life experiences						
d.	View themselves as learners and engage those with whom they work as informants						
EP 2.1.5 Advance Human Rights and Social and Economic Justice							
a.	Understand forms and mechanisms of oppression and discrimination						
b.	Advocate for human rights and social and economic justice						
c.	Engage in practices that advance social and economic justice						
EP 2.1.6 Engage in Research-Informed Practice and Practice-Informed Research							
a.	Use practice experience to inform scientific inquiry						
b.	Use research evidence to inform practice						

95

EP 2.1.7 Apply Knowledge of Human Behavior and the Social Environment							
a.	Utilize conceptual frameworks to guide the processes of assessment, intervention, and evaluation						
b.	Critique and apply knowledge to understand person and environment						
EP 2.1.8 Engage in Policy Practice to Advance Social and Economic Well-Being and to Deliver Effective Social Work Services							
a.	Analyze, formulate, and advocate for policies that advance social well-being						
b.	Collaborate with colleagues and clients for effective policy action						
EP 2.1.9 Respond to Contexts that Shape Practice							
a.	Continuously discover, appraise, and attend to changing locales, populations, scientific and technological developments, and emerging societal trends to provide relevant services						
b.	Provide leadership in promoting sustainable changes in service delivery and practice to improve the quality of social services						
EP 2.1.10 Engage, Assess, Intervene, and Evaluate with Individuals, Families, Groups, Organizations and Communities							
a.	Substantively and affectively prepare for action with individuals, families, groups, organizations, and communities						
b.	Use empathy and other interpersonal skills						
c.	Develop a mutually agreed-on focus of work and desired outcomes						
d.	Collect, organize, and interpret client data						
e.	Assess client strengths and limitations						
f.	Develop mutually agreed-on intervention goals and objectives						
g.	Select appropriate intervention strategies						
h.	Initiate actions to achieve organizational goals						
i.	Implement prevention interventions that enhance client capacities						
j.	Help clients resolve problems						
k.	Negotiate, mediate, and advocate for clients						
l.	Facilitate transitions and endings						
m.	Critically analyze, monitor, and evaluate interventions						

Chapter 13

Whose Responsibility Are Professional Ethics?

Exercise 1: Insurance Issues

Focus Competencies or Practice Behaviors:

EP 2.1.2 Apply social work ethical principles to guide professional practice
d. Apply strategies of ethical reasoning to arrive at principled decisions

GOAL: *For social workers to understand that it is incumbent on them to take measures to protect their clients.*

> Basanti Madurai has been attending the South Asia Women's Support Group for several months. After some initial resistance, her husband's family decided that it would be good for her to get out once in a while, and they have supported her attendance at the group meetings. Her mother-in-law has even been watching the children so that Basanti can attend the meetings without looking for child care. As Basanti has become more comfortable with the group, she has admitted that her husband, Prajeet, often yells at her, sometimes hits her, and has occasionally left bruises. Whenever she suggests that he might need help, Prajeet becomes very angry and says that he wouldn't have to yell and hit her if she would just do what she is supposed to. Last month they had a fight, and Basanti had to go to the emergency room for a broken arm. She was afraid that the children will become aware of the violence or that her husband would strike out at the children next, so she took the children and moved into a shelter. Prajeet was very upset that his wife and children had moved to the shelter, and he agreed to attend a treatment program. After he has completed the treatment program, Basanti is planning to return home.

Step 1: Using the problem solving tools found in figures 4.2 and 4.3 answer the following questions:

1. What is social worker Ellen Ashton's ethical responsibility in this situation?
2. If you were in Ellen's position, how would you balance your desire to protect Basanti with her right to self-determination?
3. Would your choice differ if there were no children involved?
4. Would it make a difference if you don't agree with her view that a woman's place is with her husband?
5. If you know the effectiveness or success rate of the treatment program Prajeet completed, how would that affect your decision?
6. What resources could you use as a social worker to support your position?

Step 3: Write a two page paper discussing your decision and the process you used to arrive at your decision.

Exercise 2: Friend and Colleague Dilemma

Focus Competencies or Practice Behaviors:

2.1.1 Identify as a Professional Social Worker and Conduct Oneself Accordingly
a. Advocate for client access to the services of social work
b. Practice personal reflection and self-correction to assure continual professional development
c. Attend to professional roles and boundaries
d. Demonstrate professional demeanor in behavior, appearance, and communication
e. Engage in career-long learning
f. Use supervision and consultation

GOAL: *To understand the use of peer review committees to engage in problem solving.*

> You are a social worker assigned to a satellite unit of a family service agency. You and Davis Jones, your supervisor, are the only two social workers who work in the unit. Your relationship with Davis goes back at least 15 years; he has been very important in your life at several junctions. He helped you get into social work school; he recommended you for an advanced treatment institute; and once, when your child was ill, he helped you obtain medical care from the best specialist in town. Recently, however, Davis, who is also responsible for evaluating you for pay and possible promotions, has been late arriving for work and has missed some meetings. You have had to cover for him more than a few times with his clients. You are still somewhat in awe of Davis and owe him a lot, but you suspect that his current erratic behavior may be related to alcohol and family difficulties.

Step 1: Divide into groups of 4 or 5. Each group acts as a peer review committee. Discuss the scenario above and arrive at a solution as a committee. Use figures 4.2 and 4.3 as problem solving tools.

Exercise 3: Can Deception be Justified?

Focus Competencies or Practice Behaviors:

EP 2.1.2 Apply social work ethical principles to guide professional practice
d. Apply strategies of ethical reasoning to arrive at principled decisions

GOAL: *To exam ethical decision making and accountability for professional decision making.*

> Social worker Maria Espinosa has been working for one month with Allison Bode, an extremely thin, almost gaunt, reserved 17-year-old college freshman. Allison was referred to the Family Counseling Center by her pastor after she told

him of her loneliness and obsessive thoughts. She came for help with the agreement and support of her parents. Allison is doing passing work academically but has been unsuccessful making friends at school, and for five months she has had practically no social life. This afternoon, Allison told Maria that her menstrual cycle has stopped. When Maria explored the situation, she learned that Allison is on an extremely restricted diet and exercises two to three hours a day to lose weight. She is slightly depressed but still able to concentrate on her schoolwork and reports she is seldom irritable. Based on all of this information, Maria is quite certain that Allison has anorexia and suggests she go to the college health service to consult with a physician. As soon as Allison heard the suggestion, she rejected it.

Step 1: Consult the NASW Code of Ethics regarding conflict with agency policies or relevant laws or regulations.

Step2: Define the ethical issue(s)

Step 3: Give all possible solutions to the issue(s) at hand using the NASW Code of Ethics as a guide.

Step 4: Define indicators or criteria that your agency might use to discern the quality of your ethical decision making.

Exercise 4: Client and Social Worker at Risk

Focus Competencies or Practice Behaviors:

EP 2.1.2 Apply social work ethical principles to guide professional practice
d. Apply strategies of ethical reasoning to arrive at principled decisions

GOAL: *This exercise is designed to help social workers understand the need to use agency risk audits to assess knowledge of social work ethics.*

Jeff Butz, a child protection services worker, received a call from the Community Hospital social worker. Mona Koss, a single mother with a substance abuse problem, gave birth to a baby girl two days ago. Mother and baby are due to be discharged tomorrow, but the hospital social worker does not think that the infant will be safe if she goes home with her mother. Mona, who has no permanent home, is currently living with a drug dealer who in the past has been involved in physical and sexual abuse situations.

Step 1: Divide into dyads. Review pages 269-270 in your text. What are the ethical risks associated with the scenario?

Step 2: Hold a class discussion.

Focus Competencies or Practice Behaviors:

EP 2.1.3 Apply Critical Thinking to Inform and Communicate Professional Judgments
a. Distinguish, appraise, and integrate multiple sources of knowledge, including research-based knowledge and practice wisdom
b. Analyze models of assessment, prevention, intervention, and evaluation
c. Demonstrate effective oral and written communication in working with individuals, families, groups, organizations, communities, and colleagues

GOAL: *This exercise is designed to help social worker's consider the need for agency training and consultation.*

Several months ago, Wendy Gillis told her public welfare social worker that she suspected that an upstairs neighbor, George Hill, regularly and brutally beat his 2-year-old son, Leroy. She heard the most frightful noises several evenings each week. When she saw the boy at rare intervals, he always wore bandages and looked so sad. The worker noted these remarks in her case report, but took no further action. Last month, George's wife, Anne, brought Leroy to Lakeside General Hospital emergency room. Leroy suffered from multiple fractures, which, according to his mother, occurred when he fell down the front stairs. The attending physician did not believe her story because the X-ray revealed a large number of previous fractures in addition to the current ones. As required by law, he notified child protective services (CPS) that he suspected child abuse. Andre Conti, an experienced CPS social worker, was sent to the Hill home to investigate. He talked at length with both parents, who admitted beating Leroy occasionally when he misbehaved, as their way of disciplining him. Andre suggested that there were other ways to teach a boy to behave properly but concluded that the boy was in no immediate danger. Two weeks later, another social worker made a follow-up visit to the Hill home. This worker, Millie Walker, agreed with Andre's assessment that for the time being there was no need to remove Leroy from his home. Ten days after Millie's visit, Anne Hill called for an ambulance, saying that her son was having difficulty breathing. When the ambulance crew arrived, they found Leroy unconscious. Twelve hours after he was brought to the hospital, he was pronounced dead. The postmortem confirmed that death was caused by a severe beating with a blunt instrument.

Step 1: Divide into two groups.

Step 2: Consult the NASW Code of Ethics regarding this issue. Consult your text – figures 4.2 and 4.3 to answer the following questions:

1. Did Wendy Gillis's social worker pay sufficient attention to the report of suspected child abuse and was Wendy's concern sufficient reason to warrant interfering in the Hill family?

2. How can Andre Conti or any social worker know for certain that "a clear and present danger" existed for Leroy's life?
3. When does parental discipline become child abuse?
4. Under what conditions is the removal of a child from his family justified?
5. How certain must a social worker be of the consequences?
6. Did Wendy Gillis's social worker pay sufficient attention to the report of suspected child abuse and were Wendy's concern sufficient reason to warrant interfering in the Hill family?
7. How can Andre Conti or any social worker know for certain that "a clear and present danger" existed for Leroy's life?
8. When does parental discipline become child abuse? Under what conditions is the removal of a child from his family justified?
9. How certain must a social worker be of the consequences before deciding to leave an endangered child with his family before deciding to leave an endangered child with his family?
10. How might training and consultation at the child protective services agency have changed Leroy's fate?

Step 2: Discuss your answers as a class.

Role-Play

Exercise A: Best Services for a Community

<u>Focus Competencies or Practice Behaviors:</u>

EP 2.1.2 Apply social work ethical principles to guide professional practice
a. Recognize and manage personal values in a way that allows professional values to guide practice
d. Apply strategies of ethical reasoning to arrive at principled decisions

<u>GOAL:</u> *To be aware that in addition to varying state legislation and court decisions concerning the duty to protect, a fundamental issue of concern is the assessment of the probability of violence.*

 You are a hospice social worker and have determined that her older adult client is no longer able to live alone in his home. The client responds negatively to every suggestion that the social worker has. Try various approaches to this problem situation. Keep in mind the ethical aspects.

Step 1: Divide into dyads. Review the Client Bill of Rights in your text on page 268. One student will role play the social worker and the other student will play the client.

Step 2: Discuss what happened during your role play and describe the approaches that you have defined for your client.

Chapter 13

Competencies/Practice Behaviors Exercises Assessment:

Name: _____ Date: _____

Supervisor's Name: _____

Focus Competencies/Practice Behaviors:

2.1.1 Identify as a Professional Social Worker and Conduct Oneself Accordingly
a. Advocate for client access to the services of social work
b. Practice personal reflection and self-correction to assure continual professional development
c. Attend to professional roles and boundaries
d. Demonstrate professional demeanor in behavior, appearance, and communication
e. Engage in career-long learning
f. Use supervision and consultation

EP 2.1.2 Apply social work ethical principles to guide professional practice
a. Recognize and manage personal values in a way that allows professional values to guide practice
d. Apply strategies of ethical reasoning to arrive at principled decisions

EP 2.1.3 Apply Critical Thinking to Inform and Communicate Professional Judgments
a. Distinguish, appraise, and integrate multiple sources of knowledge, including research-based knowledge and practice wisdom
b. Analyze models of assessment, prevention, intervention, and evaluation
c. Demonstrate effective oral and written communication in working with individuals, families, groups, organizations, communities, and colleagues

Instructions:

A. Evaluate your work or your partner's work in the Focus Competencies/Practice Behaviors by completing the Competencies/Practice Behaviors Assessment form below
B. What other Competencies/Practice Behaviors did you use to complete these Exercises? Be sure to record them in your assessments

1.	I have attained this competency/practice behavior (in the range of 81 to 100%)
2.	I have largely attained this competency/practice behavior (in the range of 61 to 80%)
3.	I have partially attained this competency/practice behavior (in the range of 41 to 60%)
4.	I have made a little progress in attaining this competency/practice behavior (in the range of 21 to 40%)
5.	I have made almost no progress in attaining this competency/practice behavior (in the range of 0 to 20%)

Student and Evaluator Assessment Scale and Comments	0	1	2	3	4	5	Agree/Disagree/Comments
EP 2.1.1 Identify as a Professional Social Worker and Conduct Oneself Accordingly							
a. Advocate for client access to the services of social work							

b.	Practice personal reflection and self-correction to assure continual professional development							
c.	Attend to professional roles and boundaries							
d.	Demonstrate professional demeanor in behavior, appearance, and communication							
e.	Engage in career-long learning							
f.	Use supervision and consultation							
EP 2.1.2 Apply Social Work Ethical Principles to Guide Professional Practice								
a.	Recognize and manage personal values in a way that allows professional values to guide practice							
b.	Make ethical decisions by applying NASW Code of Ethics and, as applicable, of the IFSW/IASSW Ethics in Social Work, Statement of Principles							
c.	Tolerate ambiguity in resolving ethical conflicts							
d.	Apply strategies of ethical reasoning to arrive at principled decisions							

EP 2.1.3 Apply Critical Thinking to Inform and Communicate Professional Judgments								
a.	Distinguish, appraise, and integrate multiple sources of knowledge, including research-based knowledge and practice wisdom							
b.	Analyze models of assessment, prevention, intervention, and evaluation							
c.	Demonstrate effective oral and written communication in working with individuals, families, groups, organizations, communities, and colleagues							
EP 2.1.4 Engage Diversity and Difference in Practice								
a.	Recognize the extent to which a culture's structures and values may oppress, marginalize, alienate, or create or enhance privilege and power							
b.	Gain sufficient self-awareness to eliminate the influence of personal biases and values in working with diverse groups							
c.	Recognize and communicate their understanding of the importance of difference in shaping life experiences							
d.	View themselves as learners and engage those with whom they work as informants							
EP 2.1.5 Advance Human Rights and Social and Economic Justice								
a.	Understand forms and mechanisms of oppression and discrimination							
b.	Advocate for human rights and social and economic justice							
c.	Engage in practices that advance social and economic justice							

EP 2.1.6 Engage in Research-Informed Practice and Practice-Informed Research							
a.	Use practice experience to inform scientific inquiry						
b.	Use research evidence to inform practice						
EP 2.1.7 Apply Knowledge of Human Behavior and the Social Environment							
a.	Utilize conceptual frameworks to guide the processes of assessment, intervention, and evaluation						
b.	Critique and apply knowledge to understand person and environment						
EP 2.1.8 Engage in Policy Practice to Advance Social and Economic Well-Being and to Deliver Effective Social Work Services							
a.	Analyze, formulate, and advocate for policies that advance social well-being						
b.	Collaborate with colleagues and clients for effective policy action						
EP 2.1.9 Respond to Contexts that Shape Practice							
a.	Continuously discover, appraise, and attend to changing locales, populations, scientific and technological developments, and emerging societal trends to provide relevant services						
b.	Provide leadership in promoting sustainable changes in service delivery and practice to improve the quality of social services						
EP 2.1.10 Engage, Assess, Intervene, and Evaluate with Individuals, Families, Groups, Organizations and Communities							
a.	Substantively and affectively prepare for action with individuals, families, groups, organizations, and communities						
b.	Use empathy and other interpersonal skills						
c.	Develop a mutually agreed-on focus of work and desired outcomes						
d.	Collect, organize, and interpret client data						
e.	Assess client strengths and limitations						
f.	Develop mutually agreed-on intervention goals and objectives						
g.	Select appropriate intervention strategies						
h.	Initiate actions to achieve organizational goals						
i.	Implement prevention interventions that enhance client capacities						
j.	Help clients resolve problems						
k.	Negotiate, mediate, and advocate for clients						
l.	Facilitate transitions and endings						
m.	Critically analyze, monitor, and evaluate interventions						